PROLEGOMENA
TO ANY FUTURE
METAPHYSICS

The Library of Liberal Arts
OSKAR PIEST, FOUNDER

. . . .

PROLEGOMENA
TO ANY FUTURE
METAPHYSICS

IMMANUEL KANT

With an Introduction by
LEWIS WHITE BECK

The Library of Liberal Arts
published by

Macmillan Publishing Company
New York
Collier Macmillan Publishers
London

Immanuel Kant: 1724-1804

PROLEGOMENA TO ANY FUTURE METAPHYSICS was

originally published in 1783

. . . .

Macmillan Publishing Company
866 Third Avenue
New York, New York, 10022
Collier Macmillan Canada, Inc.

First Edition
PRINTING   24 25 26 27 28   YEAR   0 1 2 3 4 5

Library of Congress Catalog Card Number: 51-10279
ISBN: 0-02-319330-1

CONTENTS

· · · · · · · · · · · · · · · ·

PROLEGOMENA
TO ANY FUTURE METAPHYSICS

NOTE ON THE TEXT

The *Prolegomena* has appeared four times in English—translated by Richardson (London, 1836), Mahaffy (London, 1872), and Bax (London, 1883), and "edited in English" by Carus (Chicago, 1902).[1] Mahaffy says that he "poured new wine into old bottles" by making extensive use of Richardson, and Carus used Mahaffy in the same way. The present edition has followed this economical plan and should be considered as only a revision—though a fairly extensive revision—of the Carus revision of Mahaffy. In emending Carus, I have made independent use of Mahaffy and Bax, and availed myself of two advantages shared with none of my predecessors—namely, the critical editions of the *Prolegomena* by Karl Vorländer (Leipzig, 1905, sixth edition, 1926) and Benno Erdmann (Preussische Akademie der Wissenschaften, 1911). The numbers in the running heads in the present edition are the page numbers of the Academy edition (Volume IV), which are appended in order to facilitate the use of commentaries, which usually, and should universally, cite that edition. I have kept the critical apparatus to a minimum, and the few footnotes which do not originate with Kant are signed with my initials or the name of the responsible editor.

Two rather significant changes have been made in the organization of the text of §§ 2 and 4. The last two sentences in the paragraph on p. 16 which begins with the sentence, "Just as little is any principle of geometry analytical," have been moved to this position from the end of the paragraph immediately following. And the five paragraphs, commencing with the words, "The essential and distinguishing feature of pure mathematical knowledge . . ." on page 17, have been moved to this position from § 4, where in the original Kant text they were included as the second to sixth paragraphs. These emendations are made following the arguments of Hans Vaihinger.[2]

[1] Some selections have been translated by C. J. Friedrich in *The Philosophy of Kant* (New York, 1950).

[2] *Kommentar zu Kants Kritik der reinen Vernunft*, I, 303; "Eine Blattversetzung in Kants Prolegomena," *Philosophische Monatshefte*, XV (1879). 321-32, 513-32.

EDITOR'S INTRODUCTION

I

Kant's *Prolegomena*—its full title, in the eighteenth-century manner, is *Prolegomena to Any Future Metaphysics Which Will Be Able to Come Forth as Science*—is a classic in metaphysics and the theory of knowledge. It deals with the perennially baffling questions: How do we know? How much can we know?

Its answers to these questions are interesting especially now. We live in one of the recurring periods of intellectual and cultural history that are skeptical and impatient of systems of speculative metaphysics, and a distrust of speculation is the leading motif of the *Prolegomena*. Though Kant's arguments against speculative metaphysics differ from those of our contemporaries, in some of his results he anticipates their negative conclusions. The *Prolegomena*, however, is not interesting merely as an historical anticipation of recent views; indeed, as such it has been as it were condemned in advance by Kant (*Prolegomena*, Introduction). Rather, its chief interest to the student of philosophy is probably the way in which it goes beyond and against the views of contemporary positivism. The book is therefore a challenge both to those who think metaphysical knowledge of the ultimate nature of things is possible and to those who regard metaphysics as comprising only pious wishes and rationalizations, "poetry," "nonsense," and "pseudoproblems."

The *Prolegomena* is, moreover, the best of all introductions to that vast and obscure masterpiece, the *Critique of Pure Reason*. It is a guide through what Kant himself calls the "thorny paths" of that work. Because of the central position the *Critique* occupies in philosophy, the *Prolegomena* thus makes a major contribution to an understanding of the chief problems of general philosophy, metaphysics, theory of knowledge, philosophy of science, and ethics. It has an exemplary lucidity and wit, making it unique among Kant's greater works and uniquely suitable as a textbook of the Kantian philosophy.

Kant was keenly aware of the difficulties and literary short-comings of the *Critique*. Even before its publication, he seems to have toyed with the possibility of presenting his ideas in a more popular and less "scholastic" form than the *Critique* was to show. From the time of the publication of the *Critique* (1781) until 1783, Kant's letters and the letters of those who were in close contact with him refer variously to the "selections," the "textbook," "the book of readings," the "summary," and the "prolegomena" that he was writing. It is probable, though it is not certain, that by 1782 Kant had composed the major part of a work for the layman, which would be introductory to the *Critique*. We believe that this work formed the nucleus of the *Prolegomena*, as published in 1783. Then his indignation was justifiably aroused by the anonymous review published in January, 1782, in the *Göttinger Gelehrte Anzeigen*. Against this he composed the Appendix to the *Prolegomena* and probably certain other sections which do not fall into the regular pattern of the exposition, but answer questions and correct misunderstandings which appeared in the review and elsewhere. Important as some of these sections are, and regardless of their date of composition, they do undoubtedly interrupt the continuity of Kant's exposition.

The student who is reading the *Prolegomena* in order to introduce himself to Kant's philosophy is therefore advised to read first, and as a connected whole, those parts of the work which are clearly parallel to the *Critique*. The following selection is recommended for this purpose:

Introduction and §§ 1, 2, 4, 5, corresponding to, and in part identical with, the Introduction and Prefaces to the *Critique*.

§§ 6-13, corresponding to (but in some respects differing from) the Transcendental Aesthetic.

§§ 14-22, corresponding to (but also differing from) the Analytic of Concepts.

§§ 23-26, 32-35, corresponding to the Analytic of Principles.

§§ 40-56, corresponding to the Transcendental Dialectic.

II

Revolutionary philosophical movements begin when a great philosopher attacks some widely held notion on which philosophy has hitherto based itself. Socrates' rejection of the notion that philosophers should study the world instead of man, Descartes' decision to doubt everything that could be doubted, and Kant's skepticism of the metaphysics which had derived ultimately from Descartes—these are outstanding examples in philosophy of Heracleitus' truth that conflict is the father of all.

Kant began as a follower of Cartesian and Leibnizian rationalism, which reached its most elaborate development in the "school metaphysics" of Christian Wolff. For it, all knowledge was or could become scientific in the rationalistic sense of the word—that is, complete, systematic, *a priori*, apodictic, and dogmatic.[1] All things in the world, whether experienced or not, were for this philosophy in principle rationally comprehensible. Metaphysics, for the followers of this tradition—and that means most of Kant's teachers and German contemporaries—was an *a priori* rational science with a degree of certainty comparable to that of pure mathematics. Though several of Kant's essays in the 1760's show a growing restiveness with dogmatic metaphysics, as late as 1770 he was, in essential points, still a rationalistic metaphysician.

In that year, on the occasion to his promotion to a professorship in the University of Königsberg, he published his Inaugural Dissertation, *The Form and Principles of the Sensible and the Intelligible World*. In this little book, he argued that space and time are "sensitive concepts," or forms in the mind which apply only to the world of sense experience or phenomena. They characterize, not the reality of things, but only their appearances. Besides them, however, the mind has certain pure "intellectual concepts"—for example, cause, substance—which do permit us to have knowledge of things as they are.

Between 1770 and 1772, Kant further extended his strictures

---

[1] "Dogmatic" in this sense refers to speculation without a prior examination of the scope and limits of knowledge. Its antonym is "critical."

on our powers of knowing reality. He decided that even the pure intellectual concepts do not apply to reality, but serve only to organize our experience of the appearances of things in space and time. In a word, by 1772 Kant had concluded that metaphysics, as this term is ordinarily used, is so far from being rational science that it is not even real knowledge at all. To demonstrate this is one of the tasks which occupied him during the following decade and which was accomplished in the *Critique of Pure Reason* and the *Prolegomena*.

There were three reasons for this renunciation of metaphysical knowledge. The *first* of these reasons was the discovery of antinomies—contradictory propositions each of which can be "proved" to be true of reality if we suppose our intellectual concepts to apply to reality at all. This "most singular phenomenon of human reason," he says, "serves as a very powerful agent to arouse philosophy from its dogmatic slumber" (*Prolegomena*, §§ 50 and 52).

The *second* reason is not made explicit in the *Prolegomena*, but is implicit throughout Kant's works. It is based on our "practical reason" or moral will, which, if it is not illusory, requires the freedom of man. But if metaphysical knowledge of reality is possible, it can arise only by extending into the world of ultimate reality those laws which are found to hold in the rational scientific study of the world of sense-experience. Among these laws is that of rigorous and universal causal determination; without this, there can be no scientific knowledge of nature. And if there is a conflict between freedom and natural causality, Kant admits that we must surrender our claim to freedom.[2]

But Kant removes this conflict through his formulation and proof of an antinomy. There is one which proves that all events occur by the necessity of nature (in accordance with the law of causal determinism) and, contrariwise, proves that there is a

[2] *Fundamental Principles of the Metaphysics of Morals,* translated by T. K. Abbott, edited by Marvin Fox (No. 16 of the "Little Library of Liberal Arts"), p. 73; cf. also "Foundation of the Metaphysics of Morals," in *Critique of Practical Reason and Other Writings in Moral Philosophy,* translated and edited by L. W. Beck (Chicago, 1949), p. 110.

"causality of freedom," that is, that there are free actions, not mechanically determined under laws of nature (§ 53). The antinomy, seen from the point of view of what it contributes to ethics, is "the most fortunate perplexity" into which human reason can ever fall.[3] For it means that rationalistic metaphysics cannot extend scientific law so far that it abrogates or even threatens the freedom required for moral responsibility. Because speculative metaphysics, instead of finally establishing causal determinism, leads to this antinomy, we are justified even theoretically in rejecting any of its conclusions as a threat to our moral concern.

Moral obligation, considered in the light of this antinomy, thus shows that scientific knowledge, however far it is pushed, can never be the whole story of reality (§ 53). Scope is allowed to another, nontheoretical and nonspeculative, activity of reason beyond the limits of the sciences of nature, and this territory must be protected against the invasion of materialism or any other speculative extension of laws of nature. Hence Kant says, "I have therefore found it necessary to deny *knowledge*, in order to make room for *faith*. The dogmatism of metaphysics . . . is the source of all that unbelief [in the presuppositions of morality], always very dogmatic, which wars against morality."[4]

The *third* reason is the one Kant has most emphasized in the *Prolegomena*. Kant had read Hume perhaps ten years before his *Inaugural Dissertation*, and after it (about 1772) his remembrance of Hume awoke him from his "dogmatic slumber."[5] Hume

[3] *Critique of Practical Reason*, translated by L. W. Beck (Chicago, 1949), p. 212.

[4] *Critique of Pure Reason*, Preface to second edition, p. xxx, translated by N. K. Smith (London, 1923), p. 29.

[5] Kant speaks as if his "dogmatic slumber" may have been twice interrupted, once by the antinomies (§§ 50, 52) and once by Hume (p. 8). He wrote Garve, the author of the anonymous review of the *Critique*, that the discovery of the antinomies was the beginning of his new work. We can only conjecture the historical relation of the discovery of the antinomies (1769) to the "remembrance of Hume" (1772). In the former year, Kant discovered that space and time did not apply to reality, but only to the phenomenal world. In the *Dissertation* (1770), Kant believed that the intellectual concepts (as

had argued that the causal connection was not a logical relation
of ideas (that is, *a* is the cause of *b* cannot be deduced from
the concept of *a*), nor, on the other hand, can it be derived from
experience, which tells us merely that *a* and *b* are usually conjoined. Its claims to be either logically or empirically justified
as a necessary principle, therefore, had to be given up. The consequence was that not only metaphysics, but also the logic of
the established sciences, was threatened, because no justification
could be found for the basic law of nature that all events have
causes. Kant discovered that Hume's problem was by no means
limited to the justification of the causal law; he found that all
the propositions claimed in metaphysics—for example, that substance is permanent, the soul is immortal, God exists—are like
the law of causal connection, in that they can be derived neither
from experience nor from logic, and yet were claimed by metaphysicians as necessary truths. Neither reasoning nor a modest
commitment to experience was therefore adequate to metaphysics.

Metaphysics, therefore, is a field where so-called "common
sense" may run riot and where flights of genius are applauded,
but where there is "as yet no standard weight and measure to
distinguish sound knowledge from shallow talk" (p. 2). In this
scholastic Babel, then, it is no wonder that Kant can say, "The
world is tired of metaphysical assertions" (Appendix, p. 126).

But the sentence just quoted continues in this manner:
"It [the world] wants [to know] the possibility of this science
[of metaphysics], the sources from which certainty therein can
be derived, and certain criteria by which it may distinguish the

opposed to the sensitive concepts of space and time) did apply to
reality, and hence that metaphysics was possible as a science. But
later, through reconsidering Hume's problem, he had to give up this
dogmatic view. That is to say, the view of space and time, which later
found expression in the first two antinomies, led first to the half-
critical, half-dogmatic position of the *Dissertation*, while the gen-
eralization of Hume's problem, which underlay the third antinomy,
forced Kant to the fully critical position of ʰhe *Critique of Pure
Reason* and the *Prolegomena*. *Cf.* Carl Siegel, "Kants Antinomienlehre
im Lichte der Inaugural-Dissertation," *Kantstudien*, XXX (1925),
67-86—especially pp. 76-77.

dialectical illusion of pure reason from truth." Why? Because the mind has a need for metaphysics—a need for final answers about the cause, nature, and end of things—which is not satisfied by the negative result of the antinomies and Hume's problem (§ 40). There is a natural predisposition for metaphysics (§ 60). "That the human mind will ever give up metaphysical researches is as little to be expected as that . . . we . . . should . . . give up breathing" (p. 116).

This, then, was the crucial situation in philosophy at the time when Kant introduced a revolution as fundamental in philosophy as that of Copernicus in astronomy.[6] Natural science, or at least the philosophical understanding of the natural sciences, was suffering under Hume's skeptical attack; the metaphysical pretensions of speculative philosophy were suffering under both Hume's attack and Kant's antinomies. Kant's problem, therefore, was twofold:

   1. *To show that mathematics*[7] *and the natural sciences are defensible against Hume's skeptical conclusions.* This he does by showing how there can be *a priori* knowledge of space and nature; that is, how there can be a system of universal and necessary truths about space and nature which, while always confirmed by experience, can never be derived from experience. The fundamental principles of such a system would be neither empirical science nor speculative metaphysics, but the only metaphysics "which can come forth as science." The "Transcendental Aesthetic" and "Transcendental Analytic" of the *Critique of Pure Reason* and most of the *Prolegomena* are devoted to this problem.

   [6] *Critique of Pure Reason,* Preface to second edition, p. xvi (translated by N. K. Smith, p. 22). Kant believed that his revolution was Copernican, not merely in caliber, but also in strategy. The student should read that Preface even if he reads no other part of the *Critique,* for this explains his "Copernican Revolution."

   [7] Hume did not usually extend his skepticism to mathematics, but, Kant believed, to be consistent with the rest of his philosophy he should have extended his skepticism even to it, and either would have had to do so if he had properly understood the nature of mathematical knowledge or else would have in principle, at least, anticipated Kant's own discoveries. Cf. *Critique of Practical Reason,* p. 127, and *Prolegomena,* §2, (2).

2. *To expose the illusions of speculative metaphysics and to substitute for them metaphysics as science*—"the science which exhibits in systematic connection the whole body (true as well as illusory) of philosophical knowledge"—which will escape the antinomies, satisfy the need of theoretical reason for a metaphysics, and yet not infringe upon our moral experience. The exposition and eradication of the illusions and his suggestions for an "immanent" metaphysics to replace them occupy Kant in §§ 40 to 56 of the *Prolegomena* and in the "Transcendental Dialectic" and part of the "Methodology" of the *Critique of Pure Reason*.

These tasks accomplished, the actual construction of a science of metaphysics is left to other works; the *Critique of Pure Reason* and the *Prolegomena* are only preparatory studies for this problem. Kant undertook to develop "metaphysics as science" in the *Metaphysical Foundations of Natural Science* [8] (1786), *Foundations of the Metaphysics of Morals* (1785), and *Metaphysics of Morals* (1797).

Having located the *Prolegomena* in the philosophy of Kant as a whole, let us turn to the argument of the *Prolegomena* to see how it accomplishes the missions assigned to it.

III

In the eighteenth century, both the rationalists and empiricists distinguished between two kinds of truth. One kind, called "truths of reason" by Leibniz and "relations of ideas" by Hume, were "logical truths," *a priori* propositions expressing necessary and universal truths which could be established by the law of contradiction (§ 2, b). These Kant calls "analytical propositions" because their predicate is found by an analysis of the subject-concept (§ 2, a). According to Hume and Leibniz, all propositions in mathematics are of this kind; [9] and, according to Leibniz, *all* true affirmative propositions (including those of both metaphysics

[8] Translated by Bax in his edition of the *Prolegomena*.

[9] This is at least Kant's view of Hume's theory (*Critique of Practical Reason*, p. 127; cf. *Enquiry Concerning Human Understanding*, IV, Pt. 1, i).

and the empirical sciences) are ultimately reducible to analytical propositions.

The rationalists and empiricists contrasted to these propositions others which they respectively called "truths of fact" and "matters of fact." These were propositions which could not be established merely by the law of contradiction and which had to be learned from experience. Since they had to be learned by observation and induction, they were contingent, only probable, *a posteriori*. For Hume, our knowledge of causal connection was such a contingent association of ideas without any objective necessity; but for Leibniz, any such "truths of facts" were evidence merely of the mind's failure to have full insight into the demonstrable necessity of the judgment. In none of these propositions could the predicate be found by analysis of the subject-concept, so Kant called them "synthetical propositions."

The rationalists and empiricists were hence in fundamental agreement that there were two and only two kinds of truths: analytical *a priori* and synthetical *a posteriori* propositions.

Kant, however, discovered that this disjunction was not exhaustive. There are also *a priori* synthetical judgments. Mathematics, natural science, and metaphysics contain such judgments (§ 2). Kant's problem, therefore, was to find out (§ 5):

1. *How* synthetical *a priori* propositions are possible in mathematics and science (for everyone, including Hume, admitted that mathematics was valid knowledge; and Hume moreover admitted the indispensability of the concept of causality, even though he could not on his principles justify its application to objects).

2. *Whether* synthetical *a priori* propositions are possible in the field of speculative metaphysics (cf. page 76 note).

Kant's argument in the *Prolegomena* is—*mirabile dictu!*—so clear that there is no need to attempt to repeat it in any simpler language. But we can summarize its main conclusions.

1. (§§ 6-13) Mathematics, especially geometry, can be *a priori* synthetical knowledge because it does not describe things as they are in themselves but only things as they appear to us. But the

form of the appearances is determined by the nature of our sensibility; inasmuch as all our sensuous experiences (which Kant calls *intuitions*) are in time or space and time, everything that we can perceive or imagine can be known *a priori* to fall under the forms of time (or space and time) and to obey their laws. Mathematics is the *a priori* elaboration of these forms of intuition presupposed in all sense-experience possible to us, and hence we can know something, *a priori* and synthetically, about all our experience. But it tells us absolutely nothing about things in themselves.

2. (§§ 14-39) Our representations (like Locke's "ideas" or Hume's "perceptions") are organized through the "association of ideas," giving rise to "judgments of perception" which are valid for us only individually, or by the understanding, giving rise to perfectly universal (nonpersonal) "judgments of experience" which are valid for all minds, that is, for "consciousness in general." [10] The result of this organization of sensuous experience by the understanding is *nature*, which is "phenomena under laws" given by the understanding. These laws, necessary for there to be any objective (that is, intersubjective) experience, are not *derived* from any experience, but are *a priori* functions or rules of the understanding which *apply* to all our experience. Kant derives

[10] §§ 19, 29. This distinction between judgments of perception and judgments of experience is generally recognized to be untenable, and Kant himself abandoned it in the second edition of the *Critique*. For it is quite clear, even in the examples that Kant gives, that judgments of perception also fall under the categories. Nevertheless, the distinction does have the value of making it more difficult to persist in the almost universal misunderstanding that Kant is writing psychology in the manner of Locke and that the categories are the way our psychical faculties work. Rather, Kant is asking us to focus on the question: "What is it that makes our experience, occurring under psychological conditions, knowledge of *objects?*" The answer is: "Its conformity to certain rules which are not rules of private association, but rules of synthesis for any consciousness whatever (consciousness in general)." It is hardly necessary to point out that "consciousness in general" for Kant does not mean a "group mind" or an "oversoul" or an absolute or divine mind, though it is one of the historical roots of these ideas which flourished in the nineteenth century.

("deduces" in the sense of giving a justification of) these laws in three steps:

a. The pure concepts of the understanding (categories) are derived from the fact that the understanding thinks only by judging; hence the logical forms of judgments are the basis of the categories (§§ 22).

b. The pure concepts of the understanding, as pure forms of judgment, are applied to the pure form of intuition (time) to give rise to the "transcendental schemata" or rules of the application of the pure concepts to whatever sense-impressions we receive (§ 34).

c. The principles, or *a priori* synthetical judgments, are universal judgments which are based on the categories and apply to the world of experience—that is, to empirical phenomena in space and time (§§ 26 and 34). These are the laws that the understanding "legislates" for nature, considered as the organization of experience.

To take the most important example, we have the hypothetical (if-then) judgment, which is the mode of judgment under the *category* of cause. This is applied to phenomena in time by the *schema* of causation, namely, the rule that the cause of a phenomenon is another phenomenon that invariably precedes it in time; and the *principle* of causation (the second "analogy of experience") is the *a priori* law that all changes of phenomena occur according to the rule of necessary connection of cause and effect. We do not know *a priori* what is the cause of any phenomenon; this must be discovered in experience. But we do know *a priori* that every event we experience does have a cause.

3. (§§ 40-57) In each case where it is admitted, even by Hume, that we have knowledge, Kant finds that this explanation is adequate. Metaphysics, however, is not an established science, so consequently Kant does not ask *how* its judgments are possible but *whether* they are possible. He finds that metaphysics, in the ordinary sense, is not *a priori* synthetical *knowledge;* for metaphysical speculation either involves the logical fallacy of "paralogism" (§§ 46 to 49), gives rise to unavoidable antinomies (§§ 50 to 54), or falls into some other error (§ 55). Hence it is

unable to give any speculative knowledge of things in themselves.

What, then, is the root of this difference between mathematics and natural science on the one hand and speculative metaphysics on the other? It lies in the fact that, in the former, the understanding applies the categories and the principles to *phenomena* within experience (thus "immanently"), while in speculative metaphysics the understanding does not restrict itself to experience but tries to know "mere beings of thought" (*noumena*) as the unconditioned grounds of all our experience and of nature itself (pp. 76, 81). Metaphysical judgments are of course, as judgments, under the categories. But in metaphysics the categories are used beyond the bounds of sense experience ("transcendently").[11] When the mind makes this use of the categories, Kant calls it *reason* instead of *understanding;* and the categories in their transcendent use he calls Ideas. This suggests Plato's use of the word, wherein the Ideas are the proper object of the metaphysician, although of course Kant does not give them the objective existence Plato is usually thought to have accorded them. The ideas for Kant (unlike Plato's Ideas) do not give rise to any metaphysical knowledge (§ 56); rather, he shows how they lead to illusions about the soul (§§ 46-49), the world (§§ 50-54), and God (§ 55).

This difference between understanding and reason, with its parallel distinction between category and Idea, is of crucial importance. It permits us to establish, in a perfectly *a priori* manner, the bounds of both theoretical knowledge and skepticism (§ 57): we can know only what can be an object of possible experience, but within possible experience we can have *a priori* synthetical knowledge. Hume's skeptical doubt as to our knowledge of nature is thereby removed,[12] while it is found to be justified as to metaphysical speculation.

[11] It is important to distinguish between "transcendent" and "transcendental." The former means "transcending the limits of experience," and hence metaphysical in the usual sense of the word; the latter means "lying at the basis of experience," and hence epistemological in the ordinary sense. Cf. *Prolegomena*, p. 122n.

[12] It has been indefatigably argued, with an acerbity unusual even in Kant-scholarship, which is notorious for the bitterness of its polemics.

4. (§§ 57-60) But because of our inveterate need for answers to questions about the nature of the soul, the freedom of the will, the existence of God, the purposes of nature, and other matters, and because we have not and cannot have any knowledge of these things, there is room for "rational faith" in God (§ 58), freedom (§ 53), immortality, and purpose (§57). This rational faith, somewhat like James' "will to believe" or Hans Vaihinger's "fictions" (§ 58) does not give us "constitutive" knowledge of objects but is of "regulative" use in directing our scientific inquiries and our moral conduct (§§ 44, 53, and 60).

5. The task of the only metaphysics that can be science,

that Kant did *not* answer Hume but simply assumed what Hume doubted—for example, the validity of the causal law—and then "rationalized" his assumption. This is indeed the impression which the *Prolegomena* makes with its "analytical method" (p. 11) of assuming mathematics and science and "regressing" upon their conditions. But the reader should keep in mind two defenses which might be made for Kant.

1. For the analytical method, the Achilles heel of Hume is his admission of the validity of pure mathematics. Granted that, Kant discovers that the conditions which make its *a priori* synthetical propositions possible will *also* justify the *a priori* synthetical judgments underlying natural science. This, however, may seem to be only "scoring a point" on Hume, not really answering him; for had he seen that mathematical knowledge was synthetical, he might have withdrawn his admission of its validity—as indeed he sometimes does with respect to geometry (cf. *Treatise of Human Nature*, II, iv).

2. The *Critique of Pure Reason* is not guilty of this appearance of circularity, for its synthetical method does not assume science and mathematics but rather establishes, by a general epistemological inquiry, principles from which they can be derived. But the justification of the principles is not merely that they produce the kind of knowledge Hume doubted; rather, they are, Kant argued, the necessary conditions also of *any* connected experience in time, of the distinction between the even apparently objective and the subjective, and of the distinction between perceptual truth and perceptual illusion which any sane man, including Hume, would have to grant. It may be that Kant fails to prove this, but he was certainly not guilty of a sophomoric *petitio principii*, which would put him in the class of the men he criticizes on p. 6. For Kant's own view of the defensibility of his procedure, see *Critique of Pure Reason*, second edition, pp. 765, 810 (Smith's translation, pp. 592, 621).

therefore, is to elaborate what *a priori* knowledge we can have; it will be metaphysics of nature if it studies the *a priori* form of what *is* (in the world of phenomena), or the metaphysics of morals if it studies the *a priori* form of obligation, of what *ought to be*. The propadeutic to this science is given in the critical eradication of claims to speculative knowledge, which results in the establishment of the "boundaries of knowledge" within which understanding has sovereignty. Because they clip the wings of speculation, yet establish the sphere of reason's theoretical and moral competence, both the *Critique of Pure Reason* and the present work are "prolegomena to any future metaphysics which will be able to come forth as science."

L. W. BECK

University of Rochester
May, 1950

SKETCH OF KANT'S LIFE AND WORK

Immanuel Kant was born in Königsberg, East Prussia, April 22, 1724. His family were among the Pietists, a Protestant sect somewhat like the Quakers and early Methodists. Pietism's deeply ethical orientation and singular lack of emphasis on theological dogmatism became a part of Kant's nature and a determining factor in his philosophy. After attending the University of Königsberg and serving as tutor in several aristocratic families, Kant became an instructor at the university. He held this position for fifteen years, lecturing and writing on metaphysics, logic, ethics, and the natural sciences. In the sciences he made significant but, at the time, little recognized contributions, especially in physics, astronomy, geology, and meteorology.

In 1770 he was appointed Professor of Logic and Metaphysics at Königsberg, and in 1781 he published his most important work, the *Critique of Pure Reason*. This work opened up new fields of study and problems for him at an age when most men are ready to retire; but for Kant there followed a period of nearly twenty years of unremitting labor and unparalleled accomplishment. Merely a list of the most important writings shows this: *Prolegomena to Any Future Metaphysics* (1783); *Idea for a Universal History* (1784); *Fundamental Principles of the Metaphysics of Morals* (1785); *Metaphysical Foundations of Natural Science* (1786); second edition of *Critique of Pure Reason* (1787); *Critique of Practical Reason* (1787); *Critique of Judgment* (1790); *Religion within the Limits of Reason Alone* (1793); *Perpetual Peace* (1795); *Metaphysics of Ethics* (1797); *Anthropology from a Pragmatic Point of View* (1798). He died in Königsberg February 12, 1804.

Kant's personality, or at least a caricature of it, is well known. Most people who know nothing else of Kant do know that the housewives of Königsberg used to set their clocks by the regular afternoon walk he took, and that his life was said to pass like the most regular of regular verbs. But a truer picture of his personality—less pedantic, Prussian, and Puritanical—comes to us from the German writer Johann Gottfried Herder:

I have had the good fortune to know a philosopher. He was my teacher. In his prime he had the happy sprightliness of a youth; he continued to have it, I believe, even as a very old man. His broad forehead, built for thinking, was the seat of an imperturbable cheerfulness and joy. Speech, the richest in thought, flowed from his lips. Playfulness, wit, and humor were at his command. His lectures were the most entertaining talks. His mind, which examined Leibniz, Wolff, Baumgarten, Crusius, and Hume, and investigated the laws of nature of Newton, Kepler, and the physicists, comprehended equally the newest works of Rousseau . . . and the latest discoveries in science. He weighed them all, and always came back to the unbiased knowledge of nature and to the moral worth of man. The history of men and peoples, natural history and science, mathematics and observation, were the sources from which he enlivened his lectures and conversation. He was indifferent to nothing worth knowing. No cabal, no sect, no prejudice, no desire for fame could ever tempt him in the slightest away from broadening and illuminating the truth. He incited and gently forced others to think for themselves; despotism was foreign to his mind. This man, whom I name with the greatest gratitude and respect, was Immanuel Kant.

                                                    L. W. B.

SELECTED BIBLIOGRAPHY

I. Collected Works

Kants gesammelte Schriften.

Published by the Preussische Akademie der Wissenschaften. Berlin, 1900-1942. 22 vols. (*Prolegomena* is contained in Vol. IV, edited by Benno Erdmann.)

Kants sämtliche Werke.

Edited by Karl Vorländer. Leipzig, 1921-1940. 10 vols. (*Prolegomena* in Vol. III.)

Kants Werke.

Edited by Ernst Cassirer. Berlin, 1912-1922. 11 vols. (*Prolegomena* in Vol. IV.)

II. German Works

Apel, Max, *Kommentar zu Kants Prolegomena. Eine Einführung in die kritische Philosophie.* Second revised edition. Leipzig, 1923.

Erdmann, Benno, *Historische Studien über Kants Prolegomena.* Halle, 1904.

Ratke, Heinrich, *Systematisches Handlexikon zu Kants Kritik der reinen Vernunft.* Leipzig, 1929.

This useful volume serves also as an index to the *Prolegomena.* It is also contained in the Vorländer edition (*vide supra*) as Vol. X.

III. Works in English

There is no work in English devoted primarily to an examination and exposition of the *Prolegomena,* but the following works will be useful in the study of the problems Kant discusses in the *Prolegomena:*

Bowers, David F., "Kant's Criticism of Metaphysics," in *The Heritage of Kant,* edited by G. T. Whitney and D. F. Bowers. Princeton, 1939. Pp. 139-159.

Ewing, A. C., *A Short Commentary on Kant's Critique of Pure Reason.* London, 1938.

Lindsay, A. D., *Kant.* London, 1934.

Paton, H. J., *Kant's Metaphysic of Experience. A Commentary on the First Half of the Kritik der reinen Vernunft,* 2 vols. London, 1936.

Paulsen, Friedrich, *Immanuel Kant, His Life and Doctrine.* Translated by J. E. Creighton and Albert Lefevre. New York, 1902.

Prichard, H. A., *Kant's Theory of Knowledge.* Oxford, 1909.

Smith, Norman Kemp, *A Commentary to Kant's Critique of Pure Reason.* London, 1918; 2nd ed. 1923. Reprinted, New York, 1950.

Walsh, W. H., "Kant's Criticism of Metaphysics," *Philosophy,* XIV (1939), pp. 313-325, 434-448.

Weldon, T. D., *Introduction to Kant's Critique of Pure Reason.* Oxford, 1945.

PROLEGOMENA

TO ANY FUTURE METAPHYSICS

INTRODUCTION

THESE *Prolegomena* are for the use, not of mere learners, but of future teachers, and even the latter should not expect that they will be serviceable for the systematic exposition of a ready-made science, but merely for the discovery of the science itself.

There are scholarly men to whom the history of philosophy (both ancient and modern) is philosophy itself; for these the present *Prolegomena* are not written. They must wait till those who endeavor to draw from the fountain of reason itself have completed their work; it will then be the turn of these scholars to inform the world of what has been done. Unfortunately, nothing can be said which, in their opinion, has not been said before, and truly the same prophecy applies to all future time; for since the human reason has for many centuries speculated upon innumerable objects in various ways, it is hardly to be expected that we should not be able to discover analogies for every new idea among the old sayings of past ages.

My purpose is to persuade all those who think metaphysics worth studying that it is absolutely necessary to pause a moment and, regarding all that has been done as though undone, to propose first the preliminary question, "Whether such a thing as metaphysics be even possible at all?"

If it be science, how is it that it cannot, like other sciences, obtain universal and lasting recognition? If not, how can it maintain its pretensions and keep the human mind in suspense with hopes never ceasing, yet never fulfilled? Whether then we

[255-256]   3

demonstrate our knowledge or our ignorance in this field, we must come once for all to a definite conclusion respecting the nature of this so-called science, which cannot possibly remain on its present footing. It seems almost ridiculous, while every other science is continually advancing, that in this, which pretends to be wisdom incarnate, for whose oracle everyone inquires, we should constantly move round the same spot, without gaining a single step. And so its votaries having melted away, we do not find men confident of their ability to shine in other sciences venturing their reputation here, where everybody, however igno- rant in other matters, presumes to deliver a final verdict, because in this domain there is actually as yet no standard weight and measure to distinguish sound knowledge from shallow talk.

After all it is nothing extraordinary in the elaboration of a science that, when men begin to wonder how far it has advanced, the question should at last occur whether and how such a science is possible at all. Human reason so delights building that it has several times built up a tower and then razed it to see how the foundation was laid. It is never too late to become reasonable and wise; but if the knowledge comes late, there is always more difficulty in starting a reform.

The question whether a science be possible presupposes a doubt as to its actuality. But such a doubt offends the men whose whole fortune consists of this supposed jewel; hence he who raises the doubt must expect opposition from all sides. Some, in the proud consciousness of their possessions, which are ancient and therefore considered legitimate, will take their metaphysical compendia in their hands and look down on him with contempt; others, who never see anything except it be identical with what they have elsewhere seen before, will not understand him, and everything will remain for a time as if nothing had happened to excite the concern or the hope for an impending change.

Nevertheless, I venture to predict that the independent reader of these *Prolegomena* will not only doubt his previous science, but ultimately be fully persuaded that it cannot exist unless the demands here stated on which its possibility depends be satisfied; and, as this has never been done, that there is, as yet, no such

thing as metaphysics. But as it can never cease to be in demand [1]
—since the interest of common sense are so intimately interwoven
with it—he must confess that a radical reform, or rather a new
birth of the science, after a new plan, is unavoidable, however
men may struggle against it for a while.

Since the *Essays* of Locke and Leibniz, or rather since the
origin of metaphysics so far as we know its history, nothing has
ever happened which could have been more decisive to its fate
than the attack made upon it by David Hume. He threw no light
on this species of knowledge, but he certainly struck a spark by
which light might have been kindled had it caught some inflam-
mable substance and had its smouldering fire been carefully
nursed and developed.

Hume started chiefly from a single but important concept in
metaphysics, namely, that of the connection of cause and effect
(including its derivatives force and action, and so on). He chal-
lenged reason, which pretends to have given birth to this concept
of herself, to answer him by what right she thinks anything could
be so constituted that if that thing be posited, something else
also must necessarily be posited; for this is the meaning of the
concept of cause. He demonstrated irrefutably that it was perfectly impossible for reason to think *a priori* and by means of
concepts such a combination, for it implies necessity. We cannot
at all see why, in consequence of the existence of one thing,
another must necessarily exist or how the concept of such a combination can arise *a priori*. Hence he inferred that reason was altogether deluded with reference to this concept, which she erro-
neously considered as one of her own children, whereas in reality
it was nothing but a bastard of imagination, impregnated by

---

[1] Says Horace:

> *Rusticus expectat, dum defluat amnis, at ille*
> *Labitur et labetur in omne volubilis aevum.*

> ["A rustic fellow waiteth on the shore
> For the river to flow away,
> But the river flows, and flows on as before,
> And it flows forever and aye".]

> *Epistle* I, 2, 42f.

experience, which subsumed certain representations under the law of association and mistook a subjective necessity (habit) for an objective necessity arising from insight. Hence he inferred that reason had no power to think such combinations, even in general, because her concepts would then be purely fictitious and all her pretended *a priori* cognitions nothing but common experiences marked with a false stamp. In plain language, this means that there is not and cannot be any such thing as metaphysics at all.[2]

However hasty and mistaken Hume's inference may appear, it was at least founded upon investigation, and this investigation deserved the concentrated attention of the brighter spirits of his day as well as determined efforts on their part to discover, if possible, a happier solution of the problem in the sense proposed by him, all of which would have speedily resulted in a complete reform of the science.

But Hume suffered the usual misfortune of metaphysicians, of not being understood. It is positively painful to see how utterly his opponents, Reid, Oswald, Beattie, and lastly Priestley, missed the point of the problem; for while they were ever taking for granted that which he doubted, and demonstrating with zeal and often with impudence that which he never thought of doubting, they so misconstrued his valuable suggestion that everything remained in its old condition, as if nothing had happened. The question was not whether the concept of cause was right, useful, and even indispensable for our knowledge of nature, for this

---

[2] Nevertheless Hume called this destructive science metaphysics and attached to it great value. "Metaphysics and morals," he declares, "are the most considerable branches of science. Mathematics and natural philosophy are not half so valuable" ["Of the Rise and Progress of the Arts and Sciences," *Essays Moral, Political, and Literary,* XIV (edited by Green and Grose, I, 187)]. But the acute man merely regarded the negative use arising from the moderation of extravagant claims of speculative reason, and the complete settlement of the many endless and troublesome controversies that mislead mankind. He overlooked the positive injury which results if reason be deprived of its most important prospects, which can alone supply to the will the highest aim for all its endeavors.

Hume had never doubted; but whether that concept could be thought by reason *a priori,* and consequently whether it possessed an inner truth, independent of all experience, implying a perhaps more extended use not restricted merely to objects of experience. This was Hume's problem. It was solely a question concerning the *origin,* not concerning the *indispensable* need of using the concept. Were the former decided, the conditions of the use and the sphere of its valid application would have been determined as a matter of course.

But to satisfy the conditions of the problem, the opponents of the great thinker should have penetrated very deeply into the nature of reason, so far as it is concerned with pure thinking— a task which did not suit them. They found a more convenient method of being defiant without any insight, namely, the appeal to *common sense.* It is indeed a great gift of God to possess right or (as they now call it) plain common sense. But this common sense must be shown in action by well-considered and reasonable thoughts and words, not by appealing to it as an oracle when no rational justification for one's position can be advanced. To appeal to common sense when insight and science fail, and no sooner—this is one of the subtile discoveries of modern times, by means of which the most superficial ranter can safely enter the lists with the most thorough thinker and hold his own. But as long as a particle of insight remains, no one would think of having recourse to this subterfuge. Seen clearly, it is but an appeal to the opinion of the multitude, of whose applause the philosopher is ashamed, while the popular charlatan glories and boasts in it. I should think that Hume might fairly have laid as much claim to common sense as Beattie and, in addition, to a critical reason (such as the latter did not possess), which keeps common sense in check and prevents it from speculating, or, if speculations are under discussion, restrains the desire to decide because it cannot satisfy itself concerning its own premises. By this means alone can common sense remain sound. Chisels and hammers may suffice to work a piece of wood, but for etching we require an etcher's needle. Thus common sense and speculative understanding are each serviceable, but each in its own way: the former in judgments which apply immediately to experience; the latter when we judge universally from mere concepts, as in metaphysics, where that which calls itself, in spite of the inappropriateness of the name, sound common sense, has no right to judge at all.

I openly confess my recollection [3] of David Hume was the very thing which many years ago first interrupted my dogmatic slumber and gave my investigations in the field of speculative philosophy a quite new direction. I was far from following him in the conclusions at which he arrived by regarding, not the whole of his problem, but a part, which by itself can give us no information. If we start from a well-founded, but undeveloped, thought which another has bequeathed to us, we may well hope by continued reflection to advance farther than the acute man to whom we owe the first spark of light.

I therefore first tried whether Hume's objection could not be put into a general form, and soon found that the concept of the connection of cause and effect was by no means the only concept by which the understanding thinks the connection of things *a priori*, but rather that metaphysics consists altogether of such concepts. I sought to ascertain their number; and when I had satisfactorily succeeded in this by starting from a single principle, I proceeded to the deduction of these concepts, which I was now certain were not derived from experience, as Hume had attempted to derive them, but sprang from the pure understanding. This deduction (which seemed impossible to my acute predecessor, which had never even occurred to anyone else, though no one had hesitated to use the concepts without investigating the basis of their objective validity) was the most difficult task which ever could have been undertaken in the service of metaphysics; and the worst was that metaphysics, such as it is, could not assist me in the least because this deduction alone can render metaphysics possible. But as soon as I had succeeded in solving Hume's

[3] [*Erinnerung*. Kant had probably read Hume before 1760, but only much later (1772?) did he begin to follow "a new direction" under Hume's influence—L.W.B.]

problem, not merely in a particular case, but with respect to the whole faculty of pure reason, I could proceed safely, though slowly, to determine the whole sphere of pure reason completely and from universal principles, in its boundaries as well as in its contents. This was required for metaphysics in order to construct its system according to a safe plan.

But I fear that the execution of Hume's problem in its widest extent (namely, my *Critique of Pure Reason*) will fare as the problem itself fared when first proposed. It will be misjudged because it is misunderstood, and misunderstood because men choose to skim through the book and not to think through it—a disagreeable task, because the work is dry, obscure, opposed to all ordinary notions, and moreover long-winded. I confess, however, I did not expect to hear from philosophers complaints of want of popularity, entertainment, and facility when the existence of highly prized and indispensable knowledge is at stake, which cannot be established otherwise than by the strictest rules of a scholastic precision. Popularity may follow, but is inadmissible at the beginning. Yet as regards a certain obscurity, arising partly from the diffuseness of the plan, owing to which the principal points of the investigation are easily lost sight of, the complaint is just, and I intend to remove it by the present *Prolegomena*.

The first-mentioned work, which discusses the pure faculty of reason in its whole compass and bounds, will remain the foundation, to which the *Prolegomena*, as a preliminary exercise, refer; for critique as a science must first be established as complete and perfect before we can think of letting metaphysics appear on the scene or even have the most distant hope of attaining it.

We have been long accustomed to seeing antiquated knowledge produced as new by taking it out of its former context and fitting it into a systematic garment of any fancy pattern with new titles. Most readers will set out by expecting nothing else from the *Critique;* but these *Prolegomena* may persuade him that it is a perfectly new science, of which no one has ever even thought, the very idea of which was unknown, and for which nothing hitherto accomplished can be of the smallest use, except it be the suggestion of Hume's doubts. Yet even he did not suspect such a formal science, but ran his ship ashore, for safety's sake, landing on scepticism, there to let it lie and rot; whereas my object is rather to give it a pilot, who, by means of safe principles of navigation drawn from a knowledge of the globe, and provided with a complete chart and compass, may steer the ship safely whither he listeth.

If in a new science which is wholly isolated and unique in its kind, we started with the prejudice that we can judge of things by means of alleged knowledge previously acquired—though this is precisely what has first to be called in question—we should only fancy we saw everywhere what we had already known, because the expressions have a similar sound. But everything would appear utterly metamorphosed, senseless, and unintelligible, because we should have as a foundation our own thoughts, made by long habit a second nature, instead of the author's. But the long-windedness of the work, so far as it depends on the subject and not on the exposition, its consequent unavoidable dryness and its scholastic precision, are qualities which can only benefit the science, though they may discredit the book.

Few writers are gifted with the subtlety and, at the same time, with the grace of David Hume, or with the depth, as well as the elegance, of Moses Mendelssohn. Yet I flatter myself I might have made my own exposition popular had my object been merely to sketch out a plan and leave its completion to others, instead of having my heart in the welfare of the science to which I had devoted myself so long; in truth, it required no little constancy, and even self-denial, to postpone the sweets of an immediate success to the prospect of a slower, but more lasting, reputation.

Making plans is often the occupation of an opulent and boastful mind, which thus obtains the reputation of a creative genius by demanding what it cannot itself supply, by censuring what it cannot improve, and by proposing what it knows not where to find. And yet something more should belong to a sound plan of a general critique of pure reason than mere conjectures if this plan is to be other than the usual declamations of pious aspirations. But pure reason is a sphere so separate and self-contained that we cannot touch a part without affecting all the rest. We can do nothing without first determining the position of each part and its relation to the rest; for, as our judgment within this sphere cannot be corrected by anything without, the validity and use of every part depends upon the relation in which it stands to all the rest within the domain of reason. As in the structure of an organized body, the end of each member can only be deduced from the full conception of the whole. It may, then, be said of such a critique that it is never trustworthy except it be perfectly complete, down to the most minute elements of pure reason. In the sphere of this faculty you can determine and define either everything or nothing.

But although a mere sketch preceding the *Critique of Pure Reason* would be unintelligible, unreliable, and useless, it is all the more useful as a sequel. It enables us to grasp the whole, to examine in detail the chief points of importance in the science, and to improve in many respects our exposition, as compared with the first execution of the work.

With that work complete, I offer here a sketch based on an *analytical* method, while the *Critique* itself had to be executed in the *synthetical* style, in order that the science may present all its articulations, as the structure of a peculiar cognitive faculty, in their natural combination. But should any reader find this sketch, which I publish as the *Prolegomena to Any Future Metaphysics*, still obscure, let him consider that not everyone is bound to study metaphysics; that many minds will succeed very well in the exact and even in deep sciences more closely allied to the empirical, while they cannot succeed in investigations dealing exclusively with abstract concepts. In such cases men should apply their talents to other subjects. But he who undertakes to judge or, still more, to construct a system of metaphysics must satisfy the demands here made, either by adopting my solution or by thoroughly refuting it and substituting another. To evade it is impossible.

In conclusion, let it be remembered that this much abused obscurity (frequently serving as a mere pretext under which people hide their own indolence or dullness) has its uses, since all who in other sciences observe a judicious silence speak authoritatively in metaphysics and make bold decisions, because their ignorance is not here contrasted with the knowledge of others. Yet it does contrast with sound critical principles, which we may therefore commend in the words of Virgil:

Ignavum, fucos, pecus a praesepibus arcent.[4]

[4] ["They defend the hives against drones, those indolent creatures" —Georgics IV 168.]

PROLEGOMENA

PREAMBLE ON THE PECULIARITIES OF ALL METAPHYSICAL KNOWLEDGE

§ 1. OF THE SOURCES OF METAPHYSICS

IF IT becomes desirable to organize any knowledge as science, it will be necessary first to determine accurately those peculiar features which no other science has in common with it, constituting its peculiarity; otherwise the boundaries of all sciences become confused, and none of them can be treated thoroughly according to its nature.

The peculiar characteristic of a science may consist of a simple difference of object, or of the sources of knowledge, or of the kind of knowledge, or perhaps of all three conjointly. On these, therefore, depends the idea of a possible science and its territory.

First, as concerns the sources of metaphysical knowledge, its very concept implies that they cannot be empirical. Its principles (including not only its maxims but its basic notions) must never be derived from experience. It must not be physical but metaphysical knowledge, namely, knowledge lying beyond experience. It can therefore have for its basis neither external experience, which is the source of physics proper, nor internal, which is the basis of empirical psychology. It is therefore *a priori* knowledge, coming from pure understanding and pure reason.

But so far metaphysics would not be distinguishable from pure mathematics; it must therefore be called *pure philosophical* knowledge; and for the meaning of this term I refer to the *Critique of the Pure Reason*,[1] where the distinction between these two employments of reason is sufficiently explained. So far concerning the sources of metaphysical knowledge.

---

[1] *Critique of Pure Reason,* "Methodology," Ch. I, Sec. 2.

§ 2. Concerning the Kind of Knowledge Which Can Alone Be Called Metaphysical

a. On the Distinction between Analytical and Synthetical Judgments in General.—The peculiarity of its sources demands that metaphysical knowledge must consist of nothing but *a priori* judgments. But whatever be their origin or their logical form, there is a distinction in judgments, as to their content, according to which they are either merely *explicative,* adding nothing to the content of knowledge, or *expansive,* increasing the given knowledge. The former may be called *analytical,* the latter *synthetical,* judgments.

Analytical judgments express nothing in the predicate but what has been already actually thought in the concept of the subject, though not so distinctly or with the same (full) consciousness. When I say: "All bodies are extended," I have not amplified in the least my concept of body, but have only analyzed it, as extension was really thought to belong to that concept before the judgment was made, though it was not expressed. This judgment is therefore analytical. On the contrary, this judgment, "All bodies have weight," contains in its predicate something not actually thought in the universal concept of body; it amplifies my knowledge by adding something to my concept, and must therefore be called synthetical.

b. The Common Principle of All Analytical Judgments Is the Law of Contradiction.—All analytical judgments depend wholly on the law of contradiction, and are in their nature *a priori* cognitions, whether the concepts that supply them with matter be empirical or not. For the predicate of an affirmative analytical judgment is already contained in the concept of the subject, of which it cannot be denied without contradiction. In the same way its opposite is necessarily denied of the subject in an analytical, but negative, judgment, by the same law of contradiction. Such is the nature of the judgments: "All bodies are extended," and "No bodies are unextended (that is, simple)."

For this very reason all analytical judgments are *a priori* even when the concepts are empirical, as, for example, "Gold is a yellow metal"; for to know this I require no experience beyond my concept of gold as a yellow metal. It is, in fact, the very concept, and I need only analyze it without looking beyond it.

c. *Synthetical Judgments Require a Different Principle from the Law of Contradiction.*—There are synthetical *a posteriori* judgments of empirical origin; but there are also others which are certain *a priori*, and which spring from pure understanding and reason. Yet they both agree in this, that they cannot possibly spring from the principle of analysis, namely, the law of contradiction, alone. They require a quite different principle from which they may be deduced, subject, of course, always to the law of contradiction, which must never be violated, even though everything cannot be deduced from it. I shall first classify synthetical judgments.

1. *Judgments of Experience* are always synthetical. For it would be absurd to base an analytical judgment on experience, as our concept suffices for the purpose without requiring any testimony from experience. That body is extended is a judgment established *a priori*, and not an empirical judgment. For before appealing to experience, we already have all the conditions of the judgment in the concept, from which we have but to elicit the predicate according to the law of contradiction, and thereby to become conscious of the necessity of the judgment, which experience could not in the least teach us.

2. *Mathematical Judgments* are all synthetical. This fact seems hitherto to have altogether escaped the observation of those who have analyzed human reason: it even seems directly opposed to all their conjectures, though it is incontestably certain and most important in its consequences. For as it was found that the conclusions of mathematicians all proceed according to the law of contradiction (as is demanded by all apodictic certainty), men persuaded themselves that the fundamental principles were known from the same law. This was a great mistake, for a synthetical proposition can indeed be established by the law of contradiction, but only by presupposing another synthetical proposition from which it follows, but never by that law alone.

First of all, we must observe that all strictly mathematical judgments are *a priori,* and not empirical, because they carry with them necessity, which cannot be obtained from experience. But if this be not conceded to me, very good; I shall confine my assertion to *pure mathematics,* the very notion of which implies that it contains pure *a priori* and not empirical knowledge.

It must at first be thought that the proposition $7 + 5 = 12$ is a mere analytical judgment, following from the concept of the sum of seven and five, according to the law of contradiction. But on closer examination it appears that the concept of the sum of $7 + 5$ contains merely their union in a single number, without its being at all thought what the particular number is that unites them. The concept of twelve is by no means thought by merely thinking of the combination of seven and five; and, analyze this possible sum as we may, we shall not discover twelve in the concept. We must go beyond these concepts, by calling to our aid some intuition which corresponds to one of the concepts— that is, either our five fingers or five points (as Segner has it in his *Arithmetic*)—and we must add successively the units of the five given in the intuition to the concept of seven. Hence our concept is really amplified by the proposition $7 + 5 = 12$, and we add to the first concept a second concept not thought in it. Arithmetical judgments are therefore synthetical, and the more plainly according as we take larger numbers; for in such cases it is clear that, however closely we analyze our concepts without calling intuition to our aid, we can never find the sum by such mere dissection.

Just as little is any principle of geometry analytical. That a straight line is the shortest path between two points is a syn- thetical proposition. For my concept of straight contains nothing of quantity, but only a quality. The concept "shortest" is there- fore altogether additional and cannot be obtained by any analysis of the concept "straight line." Here, too, intuition must come to aid us. It alone makes the synthesis possible.[2] What usually makes us believe that the predicate of such apodictic judgments is already contained in our concept, and that the judgment is therefore analytical, is the duplicity of the expression. We must

[2] [On the arrangement of the text of the remainder of this section, cf. Introduction, p. vi.—L.W.B.]

think a certain predicate as attached to a given concept, and necessity indeed belongs to the concepts. But the question is not what we must join in thought *to* the given concept, but what we actually think together with and in it, though obscurely; and so it appears that the predicate belongs to this concept necessarily indeed, yet not directly but indirectly by means of an intuition which must be present.

Some other principles, assumed by geometers, are indeed actually analytical, and depend on the law of contradiction; but they only serve, as identical propositions, as a method of concatenation, and not as principles—for example $a = a$, the whole is equal to itself, or $a + b > a$, the whole is greater than its part. And yet even these, though they are recognized as valid from mere concepts, are admitted in mathematics only because they can be represented in some intuition.

The essential and distinguishing feature of pure mathematical knowledge among all other *a priori* knowledge is that it cannot at all proceed from concepts, but only by means of the construction of concepts.[3] As therefore in its propositions it must proceed beyond the concept to that which its corresponding intuition contains, these propositions neither can, nor ought to, arise analytically, by dissection of the concept, but are all synthetical.

I cannot refrain from pointing out the disadvantage resulting to philosophy from the neglect of this easy and apparently insignificant observation. Hume being prompted to cast his eye over the whole field of *a priori* cognitions in which human understanding claims such mighty possessions (a calling he felt worthy of a philosopher) heedlessly severed from it a whole, and indeed its most valuable, province, namely, pure mathematics; for he imagined its nature or, so to speak, the state constitution of this empire depended on totally different principles, namely, on the law of contradiction alone; and although he did not divide judgments in this manner formally and universally as I have done here, what he said was equivalent to this: that mathematics contains only analytical, but metaphysics synthetical,

[3] *Critique of Pure Reason*, "Methodology," Ch. I, Sec. 1.

a priori propositions. In this, however, he was greatly mistaken, and the mistake had a decidedly injurious effect upon his whole conception. But for this, he would have extended his question concerning the origin of our synthetical judgments far beyond the metaphysical concept of causality and included in it the possibility of mathematics *a priori* also, for this latter he must have assumed to be equally synthetical. And then he could not have based his metaphysical propositions on mere experience without subjecting the axioms of mathematics equally to experience, a thing which he was far too acute to do. The good company into which metaphysics would thus have been brought would have saved it from the danger of a contemptuous ill-treatment, for the thrust intended for it must have reached mathematics, which was not and could not have been Hume's intention. Thus that acute man would have been led into considerations which must needs be similar to those that now occupy us, but which would have gained inestimably by his inimitably elegant style.

[3.] *Metaphysical Judgments,* properly so called, are all synthetical. We must distinguish judgments pertaining to metaphysics from metaphysical judgments properly so called. Many of the former are analytical, but they only afford the means for metaphysical judgments, which are the whole end of the science and which are always synthetical. For if there be concepts pertaining to metaphysics (as, for example, that of substance), the judgments springing from simple analysis of them also pertain to metaphysics, as, for example, substance is that which only exists as subject, etc.; and by means of several such analytical judgments we seek to approach the definition of the concepts. But as the analysis of a pure concept of the understanding (the kind of concept pertaining to metaphysics) does not proceed in any different manner from the dissection of any other, even empirical, concepts, not belonging to metaphysics (such as, air is an elastic fluid, the elasticity of which is not destroyed by any known degree of cold), it follows that the concept indeed, but not the analytical judgment, is properly metaphysical. This science has something peculiar in the production of its *a priori* cognitions, which must therefore be distinguished from the features it has in common with other rational knowledge. Thus the judgment that all the substance in things is permanent is a synthetical and properly metaphysical judgment.

If the *a priori* concepts which constitute the materials and tools of metaphysics have first been collected according to fixed principles, then their analysis will be of great value; it might be taught as a particular part (as a *philosophia definitiva*), containing nothing but analytical judgments pertaining to metaphysics, and could be treated separately from the synthetical which constitute metaphysics proper. For indeed these analyses are not of much value except in metaphysics, that is, as regards the synthetical judgments which are to be generated by these previously analyzed concepts.

The conclusion drawn in this section then is that metaphysics is properly concerned with synthetical propositions *a priori*, and these alone constitute its end, for which it indeed requires various dissections of its concepts, namely, analytical judgments, but wherein the procedure is not different from that in every other kind of knowledge, in which we merely seek to render our concepts distinct by analysis. But the generation of *a priori* knowledge by intuition as well as by concepts, in fine, of synthetical propositions *a priori*, especially in philosophical knowledge, constitutes the essential subject of metaphysics.

§ 3. A REMARK ON THE GENERAL DIVISION OF JUDGMENT
INTO ANALYTICAL AND SYNTHETICAL

This division is indispensable, as concerns the critique of human understanding, and therefore deserves to be called classical in such critical investigation, though otherwise it is of little use. But this is the reason why dogmatic philosophers, who always seek the sources of metaphysical judgments in metaphysics itself, and not apart from it in the pure laws of reason generally, altogether neglected this apparently obvious distinction. Thus the celebrated Wolff and his acute follower Baumgarten came to seek the proof of the principle of sufficient reason, which is clearly synthetical, in the principle of contradiction. In Locke's *Essay*, however, I find an indication of my division. For in the fourth book (Chapter III, § 9, seq.), having discussed the various con-

nections of representations in judgments, and their sources, one
of which he makes "identity or contradiction" (analytical judgments) and another the coexistence of ideas in a subject (synthetical judgments), he confesses (§ 10) that our (*a priori*) knowledge of the latter is very narrow and almost nothing. But in his
remarks on this species of knowledge, there is so little of what
is definite and reduced to rules that we cannot wonder if no one,
not even Hume, was led to make investigations concerning this
sort of proposition. For such general and yet definite principles
are not easily learned from other men, who have had them only
obscurely in their minds. One must hit on them first by one's own
reflection; then one finds them elsewhere, where one could not
possibly have found them at first because the authors themselves
did not know that such an idea lay at the basis of their observations. Men who never think independently have nevertheless the
acuteness to discover everything, after it has been once shown
them, in what was said long since, though no one was ever able
to see it there before.

§ 4. The General Question of the Prolegomena: Is Metaphysics at All Possible?

Were a metaphysics which could maintain its place as a
science really in existence, could we say: "Here is metaphysics;
learn it and it will convince you irresistibly and irrevocably of
its truth"? This question would then be useless, and there would
only remain that other question (which would rather be a test
of our acuteness than a proof of the existence of the thing itself):
"How is the science possible, and how does reason come to attain
it?" But human reason has not been so fortunate in this case.
There is no single book to which you can point as you do to
Euclid, and say: "This is metaphysics; here you may find the
noblest objects of this science, the knowledge of a highest being
and of a future existence, proved from principles of pure reason."
We can be shown indeed many propositions, demonstrably certain
and never questioned; but these are all analytical, and rather
concern the materials and the scaffolding for metaphysics than
the extension of knowledge, which is our proper object in study·

ing it (§ 2). Even supposing you produce synthetical judgments (such as the law of sufficient reason, which you have never proved, as you ought to, from pure reason *a priori,* though we gladly concede its truth), you lapse, when you try to employ them for your principal purpose, into such doubtful assertions that in all ages one metaphysics has contradicted another, either in its assertions or their proofs, and thus has itself destroyed its own claim to lasting assent. Nay, the very attempts to set up such a science are the main cause of the early appearance of skepticism, a mental attitude in which reason treats itself with such violence that it could never have arisen save from complete despair of ever satisfying its most important aspirations. For long before men began to inquire into nature methodically, they consulted abstract reason, which had to some extent been exercised by means of ordinary experience; for reason is ever present, while laws of nature must usually be discovered with labor. So metaphysics floated to the surface, like foam, which dissolved the moment it was scooped off. But immediately there appeared a new supply on the surface, to be ever eagerly gathered up by some; while others, instead of seeking in the depths the cause of the phenomenon, thought they showed their wisdom by ridiculing the idle labor of their neighbors.

Weary therefore of dogmatism, which teaches us nothing, and of skepticism, which does not even promise us anything—even the quiet state of a contented ignorance—disquieted by the importance of knowledge so much needed, and rendered suspicious by long experience of all knowledge which we believe we possess or which offers itself in the name of pure reason, there remains but one critical question on the answer to which our future procedure depends, namely, "Is metaphysics at all possible?" But this question must be answered, not by sceptical objections to the asseverations of some actual system of metaphysics (for we do not as yet admit such a thing to exist), but from the conception, as yet only problematical, of a science of this sort.

In the *Critique of Pure Reason* I have treated this question synthetically, by making inquiries into pure reason itself and endeavoring in this source to determine the elements as well as the laws of its pure use according to principles. The task is difficult and requires a resolute reader to penetrate by degrees into a system based on no data except reason itself, and which therefore seeks, without resting upon any fact, to unfold knowledge from its original germs. The *Prolegomena,* however, are designed for preparatory exercises; they are intended to point out what we have to do in order to make a science actual if it is possible, rather than to propound it. The *Prolegomena* must therefore rest upon something already known as trustworthy, from which we can set out with confidence and ascend to sources as yet unknown, the discovery of which will not only explain to us what we knew but exhibit a sphere of many cognitions which all spring from the same sources. The method of prolegomena, especially of those designed as a preparation for future metaphysics, is consequently analytical.

But it happens, fortunately, that though we cannot assume metaphysics to be an actual science, we can say with confidence that there is actually given certain pure *a priori* synthetical cognitions, pure mathematics and pure physics; for both contain propositions which are unanimously recognized, partly apodictically certain by mere reason, partly by general consent arising from experience and yet as independent of experience. We have therefore at least some uncontested synthetical knowledge *a priori* and need not ask *whether* it be possible, for it is actual, but *how* it is possible, in order that we may deduce from the principle which makes the given knowledge possible the possibility of all the rest.

§ 5. THE GENERAL PROBLEM: HOW IS KNOWLEDGE FROM PURE REASON POSSIBLE?

We have already learned the significant distinction between analytical and synthetical judgments. The possibility of analytical propositions was easily comprehended, being entirely founded on the law of contradiction. The possibility of synthetical *a posteriori* judgments, of those which are gathered from experience, also requires no particular explanations, for experience is nothing but a continued synthesis of perceptions. There remain therefore only synthetical propositions *a priori,* of which the possibility must be sought or investigated, because they must depend upon other principles than the law of contradiction.

But here we need not first establish the possibility of such propositions so as to ask whether they are possible. For there are enough of them which indeed are of undoubted certainty; and, as our present method is analytical, we shall start from the fact that such synthetical but purely rational knowledge actually exists; but we must now inquire into the ground of this possibility and ask *how* such knowledge is possible, in order that we may, from the principles of its possibility, be enabled to determine the conditions of its use, its sphere and its limits. The real problem upon which all depends, when expressed with scholastic precision, is therefore: "How are synthetic propositions *a priori* possible?"

For the sake of popular understanding I have above expressed this problem somewhat differently, as an inquiry into purely rational knowledge, which I could do for once without detriment to the desired insight, because, as we have only to do here with metaphysics and its sources, the reader will, I hope, after the foregoing reminders, keep in mind that when we speak of knowing by pure reason we do not mean analytical but synthetical knowledge.[4]

Metaphysics stands or falls with the solution of this problem;

---

[4] It is unavoidable that, as knowledge advances, certain expressions which have become classical after having been used since the infancy of science will be found inadequate and unsuitable, and a newer and more appropriate application of the terms will give rise to confusion. [This is the case with the term "analytical."] The analytical method, so far as it is opposed to the synthetical, is very different from one that consists of analytical propositions; it signifies only that we start from what is sought, as if it were given, and ascend to the only conditions under which it is possible. In this method we often use nothing but synthetical propositions, as in mathematical analysis, and it were better to term it the *regressive* method, in contradistinction to the *synthetic* or *progressive.* A principal part of logic too is distinguished by the name of analytic, which here signifies the logic of truth in contrast to dialectic, without considering whether the cognitions belonging to it are analytical or synthetical.

its very existence depends upon it. Let anyone make metaphysical assertions with ever so much plausibility, let him overwhelm us with conclusions; but if he has not previously proved able to answer this question satisfactorily, I have a right to say: This is all vain, baseless philosophy and false wisdom. You speak through pure reason and claim, as it were, to create cognitions *a priori* not only by dissecting given concepts, but also by asserting connections which do not rest upon the law of contradiction, and which you claim to conceive quite independently of all experience; how do you arrive at this, and how will you justify such pretensions? An appeal to the consent of the common sense of mankind cannot be allowed, for that is a witness whose authority depends merely upon rumor. Says Horace:

"Quodcunque ostendis mihi sic, incredulus odi." [5]

The answer to this question is as indispensable as it is difficult; and although the principal reason that it was not sought long ago is that the possibility of the question never occurred to anybody, there is yet another reason, namely, that a satisfactory answer to this one question requires a much more persistent, profound, and painstaking reflection than the most diffuse work on metaphysics, which on its first appearance promised immortal fame to its author. And every intelligent reader, when he carefully reflects what this problem requires, must at first be struck with its difficulty, and would regard it as insoluble and even impossible did there not actually exist pure synthetical cognitions *a priori*. This actually happened to David Hume, though he did not conceive the question in its entire universality as is done here and as must be done if the answer is to be decisive for all metaphysics. For how is it possible, says that acute man, that when a concept is given me I can go beyond it and connect with it another which is not contained in it, in such a manner as if the latter *necessarily* belonged to the former? Nothing but experience can furnish us with such connections (thus he concluded

[5] ["To all that which thou provest me thus, I refuse to give credence, and hate"—*Epistle* II, 3, 188.]

from the difficulty which he took to be impossibility), and all that vaunted necessity or, what is the same thing, knowledge assumed to be *a priori* is nothing but a long habit of accepting something as true, and hence of mistaking subjective necessity for objective.

Should my reader complain of the difficulty and the trouble which I shall occasion him in the solution of this problem, he is at liberty to solve it himself in an easier way. Perhaps he will then feel under obligation to the person who has undertaken for him a labor of so profound research and will rather feel some surprise at the facility with which, considering the nature of the subject, the solution has been attained. Yet it has cost years of work to solve the problem in its whole universality (using the term in the mathematical sense, namely, for that which is sufficient for all cases), and finally to exhibit it in the analytical form, as the reader will find it here.

All metaphysicians are therefore solemnly and legally suspended from their occupations till they shall have adequately answered the question, "How are synthetic cognitions *a priori* possible?" For the answer contains the only credentials which they must show when they have anything to offer us in the name of pure reason. But if they do not possess these credentials, they can expect nothing else of reasonable people, who have been deceived so often, than to be dismissed without further inquiry.

If they, on the other hand, desire to carry on their business, not as a science, but as an art of wholesome persuasion suitable to the common sense of man, this calling cannot in justice be denied them. They will then speak the modest language of a rational belief; they will grant that they are not allowed even to conjecture, far less to know, anything which lies beyond the bounds of all possible experience, but only to assume (not for speculative use, which they must abandon, but for practical use only) the existence of something possible and even indispensable for the guidance of the understanding and of the will in life. In this manner alone can they be called useful and wise men, and the more so as they renounce the title of metaphysicians. For the latter profess to be speculative philosophers; and since, when judgments *a priori* are under discussion, poor probabilities cannot be admitted (for what is declared to be known *a priori* is thereby announced as necessary), such men cannot be permitted to play with conjectures, but their assertion must be either science or nothing at all.

It may be said that the entire transcendental philosophy, which necessarily precedes all metaphysics, is nothing but the complete solution of the problem here propounded, in systematic order and completeness, and hence we have hitherto never had any transcendental philosophy. For what goes by its name is properly a part of metaphysics, whereas the former science is intended only to constitute the possibility of the latter and must therefore precede all metaphysics. And it is not surprising that when a whole science, deprived of all help from other sciences and consequently in itself quite new, is required to answer a single question satisfactorily, we should find the answer troublesome and difficult, nay, even shrouded in obscurity.

As we now proceed to this solution according to the analytical method, in which we assume that such cognitions from pure reason actually exist, we can only appeal to two sciences of theoretical knowledge (which alone is under consideration here), namely, pure mathematics and pure natural science. For these alone can exhibit to us objects in intuition, and consequently (if there should occur in them a cognition *a priori*) can show the truth or conformity of the cognition to the object *in concreto,* that is, its actuality, from which we could proceed to the ground of its possibility by the analytical method. This facilitates our work greatly for here universal considerations are not only applied to facts, but even start from them, while in a synthetic procedure they must strictly be derived *in abstracto* from concepts.

But in order to rise from these actual and, at the same time, well-grounded pure cognitions *a priori* to a possible knowledge of the kind as we are seeking, namely, to metaphysics as a science, we must comprehend that which occasions it—I mean the mere natural, though in spite of its truth still suspect, cognition [6] *a priori* which lies at the basis of that science, the elaboration of which without any critical investigation of its possibility is commonly called metaphysics. In a word, we must comprehend the natural conditions of such a science as a part of our inquiry, and thus the transcendental problem will be gradually answered by a division into four questions:

1. How is pure mathematics possible?
2. How is pure natural science possible?
3. How is metaphysics in general possible?
4. How is metaphysics as a science possible?

It may be seen that the solution of these problems, though chiefly designed to exhibit the essential matter of the *Critique,* has yet something peculiar, which for itself alone deserves attention. This is the search for the sources of given sciences in reason itself, so that its faculty of knowing something *a priori* may by its own deeds be investigated and measured. By this procedure these sciences gain, if not with regard to their contents, yet as to their proper use; and while they throw light on the higher question concerning their common origin, they give, at the same time, an occasion better to explain their own nature.

[6] [*Obgleich wegen ihrer Wahrheit nicht unverdächtige Erkenntniss.*]

FIRST PART OF THE MAIN TRANSCENDENTAL PROBLEM

HOW IS PURE MATHEMATICS POSSIBLE?

§ 6

HERE is a great and established branch of knowledge, encompassing even now a wonderfully large domain and promising an unlimited extension in the future, yet carrying with it thoroughly apodictic certainty, that is, absolute necessity, and therefore resting upon no empirical grounds. Consequently it is a pure product of reason; and, moreover, it is thoroughly synthetical. [Hence the question arises:] "How then is it possible for human reason to produce such knowledge entirely *a priori?*"

Does not this faculty [which produces mathematics], as it neither is nor can be based upon experience, presuppose some ground of knowledge *a priori,* which lies deeply hidden but which might reveal itself by these its effects if their first beginnings were but diligently ferreted out?

§ 7. But we find that all mathematical cognition has this peculiarity: it must first exhibit its concept in intuition and indeed *a priori;* therefore in an intuition which is not empirical but pure. Without this mathematics cannot take a single step; hence its judgments are always *intuitive;* whereas philosophy must be satisfied with *discursive* judgments from mere concepts, and though it may illustrate its doctrines through an intuition, can never derive them from it. This observation on the nature of mathematics gives us a clue to the first and highest condition of its possibility, which is that some pure intuition must form its basis, in which all its concepts can be exhibited or constructed, *in concreto* and yet *a priori.* If we can uncover this pure intuition and its possibility, we may thence easily explain how synthetical propositions *a priori* are possible in pure mathematics.

and consequently how this science itself is possible. For just as empirical intuition [namely, sense-perception] enables us without difficulty to enlarge the concept which we frame of an object of intuition by new predicates which intuition itself presents synthetically in experience, so also pure intuition does likewise, only with this difference, that in the latter case the synthetical judgment is *a priori* certain and apodictic, in the former only *a posteriori* and empirically certain; because this latter contains only that which occurs in contingent empirical intuition, but the former that which must necessarily be discovered in pure intuition. Here intuition, being an intuition *a priori,* is inseparably joined with the concept *prior to all experience* or particular perception.

§ 8. But with this step our perplexity seems rather to increase than to lessen. For the question now is, "How is it possible to intuit anything *a priori?*" An intuition is such a representation as would immediately depend upon the presence of the object. Hence it seems impossible to intuit spontaneously *a priori,* because intuition would in that event have to take place without either a former or a present object to refer to, and in consequence could not be intuition. Concepts indeed are such that we can easily form some of them *a priori,* namely, such as contain nothing but the thought of an object in general; and we need not find ourselves in an immediate relation to the object. Take, for instance, the concepts of quantity, of cause, etc. But even these require, in order to be meaningful and significant, a certain concrete use—that is, an application to some intuition by which an object of them is given us. But how can the intuition of the object precede the object itself?

§ 9. If our intuition were of such a nature as to represent things as they are in themselves, there would not be any intuition *a priori,* but intuition would be always empirical. For I can only know what is contained in the object in itself if it is present and given to me. It is indeed even then incomprehensible how the intuition of a present thing should make me know this thing as it is in itself, as its properties cannot migrate into my faculty of representation. But even granting this possibility, an intuition

of that sort would not take place *a priori,* that is, before the
object were presented to me; for without this latter fact no
ground of a relation between my representation and the object
can be imagined, unless it depend upon a direct implantation.

Therefore in one way only can my intuition anticipate the
actuality of the object, and be a cognition *a priori,* namely:
*if my intuition contains nothing but the form of sensibility,
antedating in my mind* [1] *all the actual impressions through which
I am affected by objects.*

For that objects of sense can only be intuited according to
this form of sensibility I can know *a priori.* Hence it follows
that propositions which concern this form of sensuous intuition
only are possible and valid for objects of the senses; as also,
conversely, that intuitions which are possible *a priori* can never
concern any other things than objects of our senses.

§ 10. Accordingly, it is only the form of sensuous intuition
by which we can intuit things *a priori,* but by which we can know
objects only as they *appear* to us (to our senses), not as they
are in themselves; and this assumption is absolutely necessary
if synthetical propositions *a priori* be granted as possible or if,
in case they actually occur, their possibility is to be comprehended
and determined beforehand.

Now, the intuitions which pure mathematics lays at the foundation of all its cognitions and judgments which appear at once
apodictic and necessary are space and time. For mathematics
must first present all its concepts in intuition, and pure mathematics in pure intuition; that is, it must construct them. If it
proceeded in any other way, it would be impossible to take a single
step; for mathematics proceeds, not analytically by dissection
of concepts, but synthetically, and if pure intuition be wanting
there is nothing in which the matter for synthetical judgments
a priori can be given. Geometry is based upon the pure intuition
of space. Arithmetic achieves its concept of number by the suc-
cessive addition of units in time, and pure mechanics cannot
attain its concepts of motion without employing the representa-

[1] [*Subjekt.*]

tion of time. Both representations, however, are only intuitions; for if we omit from the empirical intuitions of bodies and their alterations (motion) everything empirical, that is, belonging to sensation, space and time still remain, which are therefore pure intuitions that lie *a priori* at the basis of the empirical. Hence they can never be omitted; but at the same time, by their being pure intuitions *a priori*, they prove that they are mere forms of our sensibility, which must precede all empirical intuition, that is, perception of actual objects, and conformably to which objects can be known *a priori*, but only as they appear to us.

§ 11. The problem of the present section is therefore solved. Pure mathematics, as synthetical cognition *a priori*, is possible only by referring to no other objects than those of the senses. At the basis of their empirical intuition lies a pure intuition (of space and of time) which is *a priori*, because the latter intuition is nothing but the mere form of sensibility, which precedes the actual appearance of the objects, since in fact it makes them possible. Yet this faculty of intuiting *a priori* affects not the matter of the phenomenon (that is, the sensation in it, for this constitutes that which is empirical), but its form, namely, space and time. Should any man venture to doubt that these are determinations adhering not to things in themselves, but to their relation to our sensibility, I should be glad to know how he can find it possible to know *a priori* how their intuition will be characterized before we have any acquaintance with them and before they are presented to us. Such, however, is the case with space and time. But this is quite comprehensible as soon as both count for nothing more than formal conditions of our sensibility, while the objects count merely as phenomena; for then the form of the phenomenon, that is, pure intuition, can by all means be represented as proceeding from ourselves, that is, *a priori*.

§ 12. In order to add something by way of illustration and confirmation, we need only watch the ordinary and unavoidable procedure of geometers. All proofs of the complete congruence of two given figures (where the one can in every respect be substituted for the other) come ultimately to this, that they may be made to coincide, which is evidently nothing else than a synthetical proposition resting upon immediate intuition; and this intuition must be pure or given *a priori*, otherwise the proposition could not rank as apodictically certain, but would have empirical certainty only. In that case, it could only be said that it is always found to be so and holds good only as far as our perception reaches. That everywhere space (which [in its entirety] is itself no longer the boundary of another space) has three dimensions and that space cannot in any way have more is based on the proposition that not more than three lines can intersect at right angles in one point; but this proposition cannot by any means be shown from concepts, but rests immediately on intuition, and indeed on pure and *a priori* intuition because it is apodictically certain. That we can require a line to be drawn to infinity (*in indefinitum*) or that a series of changes (for example, spaces traversed by motion) shall be infinitely continued presupposes a representation of space and time, which can only attach to intuition—namely, so far as it in itself is bounded by nothing—for from concepts it could never be inferred. Consequently, the basis of mathematics actually is pure intuitions, which make its synthetical and apodictically valid propositions possible. Hence our transcendental deduction of the notions of space and of time explains at the same time the possibility of pure mathematics. Without such a deduction and the assumption "that everything which can be given to our senses (to the external senses in space, to the internal one in time) is intuited by us as it appears to us, not as it is in itself," the truth of pure mathematics may be granted, but its existence could by no means be understood.

§ 13. Those who cannot yet rid themselves of the notion that space and time are actual qualities inherent in things in themselves may exercise their acumen on the following paradox. When they have in vain attempted its solution and are free from prejudices at least for a few moments, they will suspect that the degradation of space and time to mere forms of our sensuous intuition may perhaps be well founded.

If two things are quite equal in all respects as much as can be ascertained by all means possible, quantitatively and qualitatively, it must follow that the one can in all cases and under all circumstances replace the other, and this substitution would not occasion the least perceptible difference. This in fact is true of plane figures in geometry; but some spherical figures exhibit, notwithstanding a complete internal agreement, such a difference in their external relation that the one figure cannot possibly be put in the place of the other. For instance, two spherical triangles on opposite hemispheres, which have an arc of the equator as their common base, may be quite equal, both as regards sides and angles, so that nothing is to be found in either, if it be described for itself alone and completed, that would not equally be applicable to both; and yet the one cannot be put in the place of the other (that is, upon the opposite hemisphere). Here, then, is an internal difference between the two triangles, which difference our understanding cannot describe as internal and which only manifests itself by external relations in space. But I shall adduce examples, taken from common life, that are more obvious still.

What can be more similar in every respect and in every part more alike to my hand and to my ear than their images in a mirror? And yet I cannot put such a hand as is seen in the glass in the place of its original; for if this is a right hand, that in the glass is a left one, and the image or reflection of the right ear is a left one, which never can take the place of the other. There are in this case no internal differences which our understanding could determine by thinking alone. Yet the differences are internal as the senses teach, for, notwithstanding their complete equality and similarity, the left hand cannot be enclosed in the same bounds as the right one (they are not congruent); the glove of one hand cannot be used for the other. What is the solution? These objects are not representations of things as they are in themselves and as some mere [2] understanding would know them, but sensuous intuitions, that is, appearances whose possibility rests upon the relation of certain things unknown in

[2] [In German, *pure*. The clause is meant ironically.—L.W.B.]

themselves to something else, namely, to our sensibility. Space is the form of the external intuition of this sensibility, and the internal determination of every space is possible only by the determination of its external relation to the whole of space, of which it is a part (in other words, by its relation to the outer sense). That is to say, the part is possible only through the whole, which is never the case with things in themselves, as objects of the mere understanding, but which may well be the case with mere appearances. Hence the difference between similar and equal things which are not congruent (for instance, two symmetric helices) cannot be made intelligible by any concept, but only by the relation to the right and the left hands which immediately refers to intuition.

Remark I

Pure mathematics, and especially pure geometry, can have objective reality only on condition that they refer merely to objects of sense. But in regard to the latter the principle holds good that our sense representation is not a representation of things in themselves, but of the way in which they appear to us. Hence it follows that the propositions of geometry are not the results of a mere creation of our poetic imagination, and that therefore they cannot be referred with assurance to actual objects; but rather that they are necessarily valid of space, and consequently of all that may be found in space, because space is nothing else than the form of all external appearances, and it is this form alone in which objects of sense can be given to us. Sensibility, the form of which is the basis of geometry, is that upon which the possibility of external appearance depends. Therefore these appearances can never contain anything but what geometry prescribes to them.

It would be quite otherwise if the senses were so constituted as to represent objects as they are in themselves. For then it would not by any means follow from the representation of space, which, with all its properties, serves to the geometer as an *a priori* foundation, that this foundation and everything which is thence inferred must be so in nature. The space of the geometer would be considered a mere fiction, and it would not be credited with objective validity because we cannot see how things must of necessity agree with an image of them which we make spontaneously and previous to our acquaintance with them. But if this image, or rather this formal intuition, is the essential property of our sensibility by means of which alone objects are given to us, and if this sensibility represents not things in themselves but their appearances, then we shall easily comprehend, and at the same time indisputably prove, that all external objects of our world of sense must necessarily coincide in the most rigorous way with the propositions of geometry; because sensibility, by means of its form of external intuition, namely, by space, with which the geometer is occupied, makes those objects possible as mere appearances.

It will always remain a remarkable phenomenon in the history of philosophy that there was a time when even mathematicians who at the same time were philosophers began to doubt, not of the accuracy of their geometrical propositions so far as they concerned space, but of their objective validity and the applicability of this concept itself, and of all its corollaries, to nature. They showed much concern whether a line in nature might not consist of physical points, and consequently that true space in the object might consist of simple parts, while the space which the geometer has in his mind cannot be such. They did not recognize that this thought space renders possible the physical space, that is, the extension of matter itself; that this pure space is not at all a quality of things in themselves, but a form of our sensuous faculty of representation; and that all objects in space are mere appearances, that is, not things in themselves but representations of our sensuous intuition. But such is the case, for the space of the geometer is exactly the form of sensuous intuition which we find *a priori* in us, and contains the ground of the possibility of all external appearances (according to their form); and the latter must necessarily and most rigorously agree with the propositions of the geometer, which he draws, not from any fictitious concept, but from the subjective basis of all external appearances which is sensibility itself. In this and no other way can geometry be made secure as to the undoubted objective reality of its propositions against all the intrigues of a shallow metaphysics, which is surprised at them [the geometrical propositions] because it has not traced them to the sources of their concepts.

Remark II

Whatever is given us as object must be given us in intuition. All our intuition, however, takes place by means of the senses only; the understanding intuits nothing but only reflects. And as we have just shown that the senses never and in no manner enable us to know things in themselves, but only their appearances, which are mere representations of the sensibility, we conclude that "all bodies, together with the space in which they are, must be considered nothing but mere representations in us, and exist nowhere but in our thoughts." Is not this manifest idealism?

Idealism consists in the assertion that there are none but thinking beings, all other things which we think are perceived in intuition, being nothing but representations in the thinking beings, to which no object external to them in fact corresponds. I, on the contrary, say that things as objects of our senses existing outside us are given, but we know nothing of what they may be in themselves, knowing only their appearances, that is, the representations which they cause in us by affecting our senses. Consequently I grant by all means that there are bodies without us, that is, things which, though quite unknown to us as to what they are in themselves, we yet know by the representations which their influence on our sensibility procures us. These representations we call "bodies," a term signifying merely the appearance of the thing which is unknown to us, but not therefore less actual. Can this be termed idealism? It is the very contrary.

Long before Locke's time, but assuredly since him, it has been generally assumed and granted without detriment to the actual existence of external things that many of their predicates may be said to belong, not to the things in themselves, but to their appearances, and to have no proper existence outside our representation. Heat, color, and taste, for instance, are of this kind. Now, if I go farther and, for weighty reasons, rank as mere appearances the remaining qualities of bodies also, which are called primary—such as extension, place, and, in general, space, with all that which belongs to it (impenetrability or materiality, shape, etc.)—no one in the least can adduce the reason of its being inadmissible. As little as the man who admits colors not to be properties of the object in itself, but only as modifications of the sense of sight, should on that account be called an idealist, so little can my thesis be named idealistic merely because I find that more, nay, *all the properties which constitute the intuition of a body belong merely to its appearance.*

The existence of the thing that appears is thereby not destroyed, as in genuine idealism, but it is only shown that we cannot possibly know it by the senses as it is in itself.

I should be glad to know what my assertions must be in order to avoid all idealism. Undoubtedly, I should say that the representation of space is not only perfectly conformable to the relation which our sensibility has to objects—that I have said—but that it is quite similar to the object—an assertion in which I can find as little meaning as if I said that the sensation of red has a similarity to the property of cinnabar which excites this sensation in me.

Remark III

Hence we may at once dismiss an easily foreseen but futile objection, "that by admitting the ideality of space and of time the whole sensible world would be turned into mere sham." After all philosophical insight into the nature of sensuous cognition was spoiled by making the sensibility merely a confused mode of representation, according to which we still know things as they are, but without being able to reduce everything in this our representation to a clear consciousness, I proved that sensibility consists, not in this logical distinction of clearness and obscurity, but in the genetic one of the origin of knowledge itself. For sensuous perception represents things not at all as they are, but only the mode in which they affect our senses; and consequently by sensuous perception appearances only, and not things themselves, are given to the understanding for reflection. After this necessary correction an objection rises from an unpardonable and almost intentional misconception, as if my doctrine turned all the things of the world of sense into mere illusion.

When an appearance is given us, we are still quite free as to how we should judge the matter. The appearance depends upon the senses, but the judgment upon the understanding; and the only question is whether in the determination of the object there is truth or not. But the difference between truth and dreaming is not ascertained by the nature of the representations which are referred to objects (for they are the same in both cases), but by their connection according to those rules which determine the coherence of the representations in the concept of an object, and by ascertaining whether they can subsist together in experience or not. And it is not the fault of the appearances if our cognition takes illusion for truth, that is, if the intuition, by which an object is given us, is considered a concept of the thing or even of its existence which the understanding can only think. The senses represent to us the course of the planets as now progressive, now retrogressive; and herein is neither falsehood nor truth, because as long as we hold this to be nothing but appearance we do not judge of the objective character of their motion. But as a false judgment may easily arise when the understanding is not on its guard against this subjective mode of representation being considered objective, we say they appear to move backward; it is not the senses however which must be charged with the illusion, but the understanding, whose province alone it is to make an objective judgment from appearances.

Thus, even if we did not at all reflect on the origin of our representations, whenever we connect our intuitions of sense (whatever they may contain) in space and in time, according to the rules of the coherence of all knowledge in experience, illusion or truth will arise according as we are negligent or careful. It is merely a question of the use of sensuous representations in the understanding, and not of their origin. In the same way, if I consider all the representations of the senses, together with their form, space and time, to be nothing but appearances, and space and time to be a mere form of the sensibility, which is not to be met with in objects out of it, and if I make use of these representations in reference to possible experience only, there is nothing in my regarding them as appearances that can lead astray or cause illusion. For all that they can correctly cohere according to rules of truth in experience. Thus all the propositions of geometry hold good of space as well as of all the objects of the senses, consequently, of all possible experience, whether I consider space as a mere form of the sensibility or as something cleaving to the things themselves. In the former case, however, I comprehend how I can know *a priori* these propositions concerning all the objects of external intuition. Otherwise, everything else as regards all possible experience remains just as if I had not departed from the common view.

But if I venture to go beyond all possible experience with my concepts of space and time, which I cannot refrain from doing if I proclaim them characters inherent in things in themselves (for what should prevent me from letting them hold good of the same things, even though my senses might be different, and unsuited to them?), then a grave error may arise owing to an illusion, in which I proclaim to be universally valid what is merely a subjective condition of the intuition of things and certain only for all objects of senses—namely, for all possible experience; I would refer this condition to things in themselves, and not limit it to conditions of experience.

My doctrine of the ideality of space and of time, therefore, far from reducing the whole sensible world to mere illusion, is the only means of securing the application of one of the most important kinds of knowledge (that which mathematics propounds *a priori*) to actual objects and of preventing its being regarded as mere illusion. For without this observation it would be quite impossible to make out whether the intuitions of space and time, which we borrow from no experience and which yet lie in our representation *a priori,* are not mere phantasms of our brain to which objects do not correspond, at least not adequately; and, consequently, whether we have been able to show its unquestionable validity with regard to all the objects of the sensible world just because they are mere appearances.

Secondly, though these my principles make appearances of the representations of the senses, they are so far from turning the truth of experience into mere illusion that they are rather the only means of preventing the transcendental illusion, by which metaphysics has hitherto been deceived and led to the childish endeavor of catching at bubbles, because appearances, which are mere representations, were taken for things in themselves. Here originated the remarkable occurrence of the antinomy of reason which I shall mention later and which is solved by the single observation that appearance, as long as it is employed in experience, produces truth; but the moment it transgresses the bounds of experience, and consequently becomes transcendent, produces nothing but illusion.

Inasmuch, therefore, as I leave to things as we obtain them by the senses their actuality and only limit our sensuous intuition of these things to this: that it represents in no respect, not even in the pure intuitions of space and of time, anything more than mere appearance of those things, but never their constitution in themselves, this is not a sweeping illusion invented for nature by me. My protestation, too, against all charges of idealism is so valid and clear as even to seem superfluous, were there not incompetent judges who, while they would have an old name for every deviation from their perverse though common opinion and never judge of the spirit of philosophic nomenclature, but cling to the letter only, are ready to put their own conceits in the place of well-defined notions, and thereby deform and distort them. I have myself given this my theory the name of transcendental idealism, but that cannot authorize anyone to confound it either with the empirical idealism of Descartes (indeed, his was only an insoluble problem, owing to which he thought everyone at liberty to deny the existence of the corporeal world because it could never be proved satisfactorily), or with the mystical and visionary idealism of Berkeley, against which and other similar phantasms our *Critique* contains the proper antidote. My idealism concerns not the existence of things (the doubting of which, however, constitutes idealism in the ordinary sense), since it never came into my head to doubt it, but it concerns the sensuous representation of things to which space and time especially belong. Of these [namely, space and time], consequently of all appearances in general, I have only shown that they are neither things (but mere modes of representation) nor determinations belonging to things in themselves. But the word "transcendental," which with me never means a reference of our knowledge to things, but only to the cognitive faculty, was meant to obviate this misconception. Yet rather than give further occasion to it by this word, I now retract it and desire this idealism of mine to be called "critical." But if it be really an objectionable idealism to convert actual things (not appearances) into mere representations, by what name shall we call him who conversely changes mere representations to things? It may, I think, be called "dreaming idealism," in contradistinction to the former, which may be called "visionary," both of which are to be refuted by my transcendental or, better, *critical* idealism.

SECOND PART OF THE MAIN TRANSCEN-
DENTAL PROBLEM

HOW IS PURE SCIENCE OF NATURE POSSIBLE?

§ 14

NATURE is the existence of things, so far as it is determined according to universal laws. Should nature signify the existence of things in themselves, we could never know it either *a priori* or *a posteriori*. Not *a priori,* for how can we know what belongs to things in themselves, since this never can be done by the dissection of our concepts (in analytical propositions)? For I do not want to know what is contained in my concept of a thing (for that belongs to its logical essence), but what in the actuality of the thing is superadded to my concept and by which the thing itself is determined in its existence apart from the concept. My understanding and the conditions on which alone it can connect the determination of things in their existence do not prescribe any rule to things [in] themselves; these do not conform to my understanding, but it would have to conform itself to them; they would therefore have to be first given me in order to gather these determinations from them, wherefore they would not be known *a priori.*

But knowledge of the nature of things in themselves *a posteriori* would be equally impossible. For, if experience is to teach us laws to which the existence of things is subject, these laws, if they have reference to things in themselves, would have to hold them of necessity even outside our experience. But experience teaches us what exists and how it exists, but never that it must necessarily exist so and not otherwise. Experience therefore can never teach us the nature of things in themselves.

§ 15.   We nevertheless actually possess a pure science of na-

42   [294]

ture in which are propounded, *a priori* and with all the necessity requisite to apodictical propositions, laws to which nature is subject. I need only call to witness that propaedeutic of natural science which, under the title of the universal science of nature, precedes all physics (which is founded upon empirical principles). In it we have mathematics applied to appearances, and also merely discursive principles (or those derived from concepts), which constitute the philosophical part of the pure knowledge of nature. But there are several things in it which are not quite pure and independent of empirical sources, such as the concept of *motion,* that of *impenetrability* (upon which the empirical concept of matter rests), that of *inertia,* and many others, which prevent its being called a perfectly pure science of nature. Besides, it only refers to objects of the outer sense, and therefore does not give an example of a universal science of nature, in the strict sense, for such a science must bring nature in general, whether it regards the object of the outer or that of the inner sense (the object of physics as well as psychology), under universal laws. But among the principles of this universal physics there are a few which actually have the required universality; for instance, the propositions that "substance is permanent," that "every event is determined by a cause according to constant laws," etc. These are actually universal laws of nature, which hold completely *a priori.* There is then in fact a pure science of nature, and the question arises, *How is it possible?*

§ 16. The word *nature* assumes yet another meaning which defines the object, whereas in the former sense it only denotes the conformity to law of the determinations of the existence of things generally. If we consider it *materialiter,* "nature is the complex of all the objects of experience." And with this only are we now concerned, for anyhow things which can never be objects of experience, if they had to be known as to their nature, would oblige us to have recourse to concepts whose meaning could never be given *in concreto* (by any example of possible experience). Consequently we would have to form for ourselves a list of concepts of their nature, the reality whereof could never be determined. That is, we could never learn whether they actually referred to objects or were mere creations of thought. The knowledge of what cannot be an object of experience would be hyperphysical, and with things hyperphysical we are here not concerned, but only with the knowledge of nature, the actuality of which can be confirmed by experience, though this knowledge is possible *a priori* and precedes all experience.

§ 17. The formal aspect of nature in this narrower sense is therefore the conformity to law of all the objects of experience and, so far as it is known *a priori,* their *necessary* conformity. But it has just been shown that the laws of nature can never be known *a priori* in objects so far as they are considered, not in reference to possible experience, but as things in themselves. And our inquiry here extends, not to things in themselves (the properties of which we pass by), but to things as objects of possible experience, and the complex of these is what we here properly designate as nature. And now I ask, when the possibility of knowledge of nature *a priori* is in question, whether it is better to arrange the problem thus: "How can we know *a priori* that things as objects of experience necessarily conform to law?" or thus: "How is it possible to know *a priori* the necessary conformity to law of experience itself as regards all its objects generally?"

Closely considered, the solution of the problem represented in either way amounts, with regard to the pure knowledge of nature (which is the point of the question at issue), entirely to the same thing. For the subjective laws, under which alone an empirical knowledge of things is possible, hold good of these things as objects of possible experience (not as things in themselves, which are not considered here). It is all the same whether I say: "A judgment of perception can never rank as experience without the law that, whenever an event is observed, it is always referred to some antecedent, which it follows according to a universal rule," or: "Everything of which experience teaches that it happens must have a cause."

It is, however, more suitable to choose the first formula. For we can *a priori* and prior to all given objects have a knowledge of those conditions on which alone experience of them is possible, but never of the laws to which things may in themselves be subject, without reference to possible experience. We cannot, therefore, study the nature of things *a priori* otherwise than by investigating the conditions and the universal (though subjective) laws, under which alone such a cognition as experience (as to mere form) is possible, and we determine accordingly the possibility of things as objects of experience. For if I should choose the second formula and seek the *a priori* conditions under which nature as an object of experience is possible, I might easily fall into error and fancy that I was speaking of nature as a thing in itself, and then move round in endless circles, in a vain search for laws concerning things of which nothing is given me.

Accordingly, we shall here be concerned with experience only and the universal conditions of its possibility, which are given *a priori*. Thence we shall define nature as the whole object of all possible experience. I think it will be understood that I here do not mean the rules of the observation of a nature that is already given, for these already presuppose experience. Thus I do not mean how (through experience) we can study the laws of nature, for these would not then be laws *a priori* and would yield us no pure science of nature; but [I mean to ask] how the conditions *a priori* of the possibility of experience are at the same time the sources from which all universal laws of nature must be derived.

§ 18. In the first place we must state that, while all judgments of experience are empirical (that is, have their ground in immediate sense-perception), all empirical judgments are not judgments of experience; but, besides the empirical, and in general besides what is given to the sensuous intuition, special concepts must yet be superadded—concepts which have their origin wholly *a priori* in the pure understanding, and under which every perception must be first of all subsumed and then by their means changed into experience.

Empirical judgments, so far as they have objective validity, are *judgments of experience*, but those which are only subjectively valid I name mere *judgments of perception*. The latter require no pure concept of the understanding, but only the logical connection of perception in a thinking subject. But the former always require, besides the representation of the sensuous intuition, special *concepts originally begotten in the understanding,* which make possible the objective validity of the judgment of experience.

All our judgments are at first merely judgments of perception; they hold good only for us (that is, for our subject), and we do not till afterward give them a new reference (to an object) and desire that they shall always hold good for us and in the same way for everybody else; for when a judgment agrees with an object, all judgments concerning the same object must likewise agree among themselves, and thus the objective validity of the judgment of experience signifies nothing else than its necessary universal validity. And conversely when we have ground for considering a judgment as necessarily having universal validity (which never depends upon perception, but upon the pure concept of the understanding under which the perception is subsumed), we must consider that it is objective also—that is, that it expresses not merely a reference of our perception to a subject, but a characteristic of the object. For there would be no reason for the judgments of other men necessarily agreeing with mine if it were not the unity of the object to which they all refer and with which they accord; hence they must all agree with one another.

§ 19. Therefore objective validity and necessary universality (for everybody) are equivalent terms, and though we do not know the object in itself, yet when we consider a judgment as universal, and hence necessary, we thereby understand it to have objective validity. By this judgment we know the object (though it remains unknown as it is in itself) by the universal and necessary connection of the given perceptions. As this is the case with all objects of sense, judgments of experience take their objective validity, not from the immediate knowledge of the object (which is impossible), but from the condition of universal validity of empirical judgments, which, as already said, never rests upon empirical or, in short, sensuous conditions, but upon a pure concept of the understanding. The object in itself always remains unknown; but when by the concept of the understanding the connection of the representations of the object, which it gives to our sensibility, is determined as universally valid, the object is determined by this relation, and the judgment is objective.

To illustrate the matter: when we say, "The room is warm, sugar sweet, and wormwood bitter," [1] we have only subjectively valid judgments. I do not at all expect that I or any other person shall always find it as I now do; each of these sentences only expresses a relation of two sensations to the same subject, that is, myself, and that only in my present state of perception; consequently they are not valid of the object. Such are judgments of perception. Judgments of experience are of quite a different nature. What experience teaches me under certain circumstances, it must always teach me and everybody; and its validity is not limited to the subject nor to its state at a particular time. Hence I pronounce all such judgments objectively valid. For instance, when I say the air is elastic, this judgment is as yet a judgment of perception only; I do nothing but refer two of my sensations to each other. But if I would have it called a judgment of experience, I require this connection to stand under a condition which makes it universally valid. I desire therefore that I and everybody else should always connect necessarily the same perceptions under the same circumstances.

§ 20. We must consequently analyze experience in general in order to see what is contained in this product of the senses and of the understanding, and how the judgment of experience itself is possible. The foundation is the intuition of which I become

---

[1] I freely grant that these examples do not represent such judgments of perception as ever could become judgments of experience, even though a concept of the understanding were superadded, because they refer merely to feeling, which everybody knows to be merely subjective and which of course can never be attributed to the object, and consequently never become objective. I only wished to give here an example of a judgment that is merely subjectively valid, containing no ground for necessary universal validity and thereby for a relation to the object. An example of the judgments of perception which become judgments of experience by superadded concepts of the understanding will be given in the next note.

conscious, that is, perception (*perceptio*), which pertains merely to the senses. But in the next place, there is judging (which belongs only to the understanding). But this judging may be twofold: first, I may merely compare perceptions and connect them in a consciousness of my particular state; or, secondly, I may connect them in consciousness in general. The former judgment is merely a judgment of perception, and hence is of subjective validity only; it is merely a connection of perceptions in my mental state, without reference to the object. Hence it does not, as is commonly imagined, suffice for experience that perceptions are compared and connected in consciousness through judgment; thence arises no universal validity and necessity by virtue of which alone consciousness [2] can be objectively valid, that is, can be called experience.

Quite another judgment therefore is required before perception can become experience. The given intuition must be subsumed under a concept which determines the form of judging in general relatively to the intuition, connects empirical consciousness of intuition in consciousness in general, and thereby procures universal validity for empirical judgments. A concept of this nature is a pure *a priori* concept of the understanding, which does nothing but determine for an intuition the general way in which it can be used for judgments. Let the concept be that of cause; then it determines the intuition which is subsumed under it, for example, that of air, relative to judging in general—namely, the concept of air in respect to its expansion serves in the relation of antecedent to consequent in a hypothetical judgment. The concept of cause accordingly is a pure concept of the understanding, which is totally disparate from all possible perception and only serves to determine the representation subsumed under it, with respect to judging in general, and so to make a universally valid judgment possible.

Before, therefore, a judgment of perception can become a judgment of experience, it is requisite that the perception should be subsumed under some such concept of the understanding; for

[2] [Or "judgment."—L.W.B.]

instance, air belongs under the concept of cause, which determines our judgment about it in respect to its expansion as hypothetical.[3] Thereby the expansion of the air is represented, not as
merely belonging to the perception of the air in my present state
or in several states of mine, or in the perceptual state of others,
but as belonging to it necessarily. The judgment, "Air is elastic,"
becomes universally valid and a judgment of experience only because certain judgments precede it which subsume the intuition
of air under the concept of cause and effect; and they thereby
determine the perceptions, not merely with respect to one another
in me, but with respect to the form of judging in general (which
is here hypothetical), and in this way they render the empirical
judgment universally valid.

If all our synthetical judgments are analyzed so far as they
are objectively valid, it will be found that they never consist of
mere intuitions connected only (as is commonly believed) by
comparison into a judgment; but that they would be impossible
were not a pure concept of the understanding superadded to the
concepts abstracted from intuition, under which concept these
latter are subsumed and in this manner only combined into an
objectively valid judgment. Even the judgments of pure mathematics in their simplest axioms are not exempt from this condition. The principle, "A straight line is the shortest distance beween
two points," presupposes that the line is subsumed under the
concept of magnitude, which certainly is no mere intuition, but
has its seat in the understanding alone and serves to determine
the intuition (of the line) with regard to the judgments which
may be made about it, in respect to their quantity, that is, to

[3] As an easier example, we may take the following: "When the sun
shines on the stone, it grows warm." This judgment, however often I
and others may have perceived it, is a mere judgment of perception
and contains no necessity; perceptions are only usually conjoined in
this manner. But if I say, "The sun warms the stone," I add to the
perception a concept of the understanding, namely, that of cause,
which necessarily connects with the concept of sunshine that of heat,
and the synthetical judgment becomes of necessity universally valid.
namely, objective, and is converted from a perception into experience.

plurality (as *judicia plurativa*).⁴ For under them it is understood that in a given intuition there is contained a plurality of homogeneous parts.

§ 21.   To prove, then, the possibility of experience so far as it rests upon pure concepts of the understanding *a priori,* we must first represent what belongs to judging in general and the various functions of the understanding in a complete table. For the pure concepts of the understanding must run parallel to these functions, as such concepts are nothing more than concepts of intuitions in general, so far as these are determined by one or other of these functions of judging, in themselves, that is, necessarily and universally. Hereby also the *a priori* principles of the possibility of all experience, as objectively valid empirical knowledge, will be precisely determined. For they are nothing but propositions which subsume all perception (under certain universal conditions of intuition) under those pure concepts of the understanding.

LOGICAL TABLE OF JUDGMENTS

1 *As to Quantity*	2 *As to Quality*
Universal	Affirmative
Particular	Negative
Singular	Infinite

3 *As to Relation*	4 *As to Modality*
Categorical	Problematic
Hypothetical	Assertoric
Disjunctive	Apodictic

⁴ This name seems preferable to the term *particularia*, which is used for these judgments in logic. For the latter implies the idea that they are not universal. But when I start from unity (in singular judgments) and so proceed to totality, I must not [even indirectly and negatively] imply any reference to totality. I think plurality merely without totality, and not the exception from totality. This is necessary if logical distinctions are to form the basis of the pure concepts of the understanding. However, logical usage need not be changed.

TRANSCENDENTAL TABLE OF THE CONCEPTS OF THE UNDERSTANDING

I *As to Quantity* Unity (Measure) Plurality (Magnitude) Totality (Whole)	2 *As to Quality* Reality Negation Limitation
3 *As to Relation* Substance Cause Community	4 *As to Modality* Possibility Existence Necessity

PURE PHYSICAL [5] TABLE OF THE UNIVERSAL PRINCIPLES OF THE SCIENCE OF NATURE

I Axioms of Intuition	2 Anticipations of Perception
3 Analogies of Experience	4 Postulates of Empirical Thinking Generally

§ 21*a*. In order to comprise the whole matter in one idea, it is first necessary to remind the reader that we are discussing, not the origin of experience, but that which lies in experience. The former pertains to empirical psychology and would even then never be adequately explained without the latter, which belongs to the critique of knowledge, and particularly of the understanding.

Experience consists of intuitions, which belong to the sensibility, and of judgments, which are entirely a work of the understanding. But the judgments which the understanding forms solely

[5] [Kant uses the term *physiological* in its etymological meaning as "pertaining to the science of physics," that is, nature in general, not as we use the term now as "pertaining to the function of the living body." Accordingly, it has been translated as *physical*.—Carus.]

from sensuous intuitions are far from being judgments of experience. For in the one case the judgment connects only the perceptions as they are given in sensuous intuition, while in the other the judgments must express what experience in general and not what the mere perception (which possesses only subjective validity) contains. The judgment of experience must therefore add to the sensuous intuition and its logical connection in a judgment (after it has been rendered universal by comparison) something that determines the synthetical judgment as necessary and therefore as universally valid. This can be nothing else than that concept which represents the intuition as determined in itself with regard to one form of judgment rather than another, namely, a concept of that synthetical unity of intuitions which can only be represented by a given logical function of judgments.

§ 22.   The sum of the matter is this: the business of the senses is to intuit, that of the understanding is to think. But thinking is uniting representations in one consciousness. This union originates either merely relative to the subject and is accidental and subjective, or takes place absolutely and is necessary or objective. The union of representations in one consciousness is judgment. Thinking, therefore, is the same as judging or referring representations to judgments in general. Hence judgments are either merely subjective, when representations are referred to a consciousness in one subject only and united in it, or objective, when they are united in consciousness in general, that is, necessarily. The logical functions of all judgments are but various modes of uniting representations in consciousness. But if they serve for concepts, they are concepts of the necessary union of representations in [any] consciousness, and so are principles of objectively valid judgments. This union in consciousness is either analytical, by identity, or synthetical, by the combination and addition of various representations one to another. Experience consists in the synthetical connection of phenomena (perceptions) in consciousness, so far as this connection is necessary. Hence the pure concepts of the understanding are those under which all perceptions must be subsumed ere they can serve for judgments of experience, in which the synthetical unity of the perceptions is represented as necessary and universally valid.[6]

§ 23.   Judgments, when considered merely as the condition of the union of given representations in a consciousness, are rules. These rules, so far as they represent the union as necessary, are rules *a priori*, and, insofar as they cannot be deduced from higher rules, are principles. But in regard to the possibility of all experience, merely in relation to the form of thinking in it, no conditions of judgments of experience are higher than those which bring the appearances, according to the various form of their intuition, under pure concepts of the understanding, which render the empirical judgment objectively valid. These are therefore the *a priori* principles of possible experience.

The principles of possible experience are then at the same time universal laws of nature, which can be known *a priori*. And thus the problem of our second question, "How is the pure science of nature possible?" is solved. For the system which is required for the form of a science is to be met with in perfection here, because, beyond the above-mentioned formal conditions of all judgments in general (and hence of all rules in general) offered in logic, no others are possible, and these constitute a logical system. The concepts grounded thereupon, which contain the *a priori* conditions of all synthetical and necessary judgments, accordingly constitute a transcendental system. Finally the principles, by means of which all phenomena are subsumed under

---

[6] But how does the proposition that judgments of experience contain necessity in the synthesis of perceptions agree with my statement so often before inculcated that experience as cognition *a posteriori* can afford contingent judgments only? When I say that experience teaches me something, I mean only the perception that lies in experience—for example, that heat always follows the shining of the sun on a stone; consequently the proposition of experience is always so far accidental. That this heat necessarily follows the shining of the sun is contained indeed in the judgment of experience (by means of the concept of cause), yet is a fact not learned by experience; for conversely, experience is first of all generated by this addition of the concept of the understanding (of cause) to perception. How perception attains this addition may be seen by referring in the *Critique* itself to the [first] section of the "Transcendental Faculty of Judgment."

these concepts, constitute a physical system, that is, a system of nature, which precedes all empirical knowledge of nature, and makes it possible. It may in strictness be denominated the universal and pure science of nature.

§ 24. The first of the physical principles subsumes all phenomena, as intuitions in space and time, under the concept of quantity, and is thus a principle of the application of mathematics to experience. The second one subsumes the strictly empirical element, namely, sensation, which denotes the real in intuitions, not indeed directly under the concept of quantity, because sensation is not an intuition that *contains* either space or time, though it places the respective object corresponding to it in both. But still there is between reality (sense-representation) and the zero, or total void of intuition in time, a difference which has a quantity. For between every given degree of light and of darkness, between every degree of heat and of absolute cold, between every degree of weight and of absolute lightness, between every degree of occupancy space and of totally void space, diminishing degrees can be conceived, in the same manner as between consciousness and total unconsciousness (psychological darkness) ever-diminishing degrees obtain. Hence there is no perception that can prove an absolute absence; for instance, no psychological darkness that cannot be considered as consciousness which is only outbalanced by a stronger consciousness. This occurs in all cases of sensation, and so the understanding can anticipate even sensations, which constitute the peculiar quality of empirical representations (appearances), by means of the principle that they all have degree (and consequently that what is real in all appearance has degree). Here is the second application of mathematics (*mathesis intensorum*) to the science of nature.

§ 25. Anent the relation of appearances merely with a view to their existence, the determination of the relation is not mathematical but dynamical, and can never be objectively valid, consequently never fit for experience, if it does not come under *a priori* principles by which the empirical knowledge relative to appearances first becomes possible. Hence appearances must be subsumed under the concept of substance, which as a concept of a thing is the foundation of all determination of existence; or, secondly—so far as a succession is found among appearances, that is, an event—under the concept of an effect with reference to cause; or lastly—so far as coexistence is to be known objectively, that is, by a judgment of experience—under the concept of community (action and reaction). Thus *a priori* principles form the basis of objectively valid, though empirical, judgments—that is, of the possibility of experience so far as it must connect objects as existing in nature. These principles are the real laws of nature, which may be termed "dynamical."

Finally knowledge of the agreement and connection, not only of appearances among themselves in experience, but of their relation to experience in general, belongs to the judgments of experience. This relation contains either their agreement with the formal conditions, which the understanding recognizes, or their coherence with the materials of the senses and of perception, or combines both into one concept. Consequently, their relation to experience in general entails possibility, actuality, and necessity, according to universal laws of nature. This would constitute the physical doctrine of method for distinguishing truth from hypotheses and for determining the limits of certainty of the latter.

§ 26. The third table of principles drawn by the critical method from the nature of the understanding itself shows an inherent perfection, which raises it far above every other table which has hitherto, though in vain, been tried or may yet be tried by analyzing the objects themselves dogmatically. It exhibits all synthetical *a priori* principles completely and according to one principle, namely, the faculty of judging in general, constituting the essence of experience as regards the understanding; so that we can be certain that there are no more such principles. This affords a satisfaction which can never be attained by the dogmatic method. Yet this is not all; there is a still greater merit in it.

We must carefully bear in mind the premise which shows the possibility of this cognition *a priori* and, at the same time, limits all such principles to a condition which must never be lost sight of if we desire it not to be misunderstood and extended in use beyond the original sense which the understanding attaches to it.

This limit is that they contain nothing but the conditions of possible experience in general so far as it is subjected to laws *a priori*. Consequently, I do not say that things *in themselves* possess a magnitude; that their reality possesses a degree, their existence a connection of accidents in a substance, etc. This nobody can prove, because such a synthetical connection from mere concepts, without any reference to sensuous intuition on the one side or connection of it in a possible experience on the other, is absolutely impossible. The essential limitation of the concepts in these principles then is that all things *as objects of experience only* stand necessarily *a priori* under the aforementioned conditions.

Hence there follows, secondly, a specifically peculiar mode of proof of these principles; they are not directly referred to appearances and to their relation, but to the possibility of experience, of which appearances constitute the matter only, not the form. Thus they are referred to objectively and universally valid synthetical propositions, in which we distinguish judgments of experience from those of perception. This takes place because appearances, as mere intuitions *occupying a part of space and time,* come under the concept of quantity, which synthetically unites their multiplicity *a priori* according to rules. Again, insofar as the perception contains, besides intuition, sensation, and between the latter and nothing (that is, the total disappearance of sensation), there is an ever-decreasing transition, it is apparent that the real within appearances must have a degree, so far as it (namely, the sensation) *does not itself occupy any part of space or of time.*[7] Still the transition to this real from empty time or

[7] Heat and light are in a small space just as large, as to degree, as in a large one; in like manner the internal representations, pain, consciousness generally, whether they last a short or a long time, need not vary as to the degree. Hence the quantity is here in a point and in a moment just as great as in any space or time, however great. Degrees are quantities not in intuition, but in mere sensation (or the quantity of the content [*Grundes*] of an intuition). Hence they can only be estimated quantitatively by the relation of 1 to 0, namely, by their capability of decreasing by infinite intermediate degrees to disappearance, or of increasing from naught through infinite gradations to a determinate sensation in a certain time. *Quantitas qualitatis est gradus.* "The quantity of quality is degree."

empty space is possible only in time. Consequently, although sensation, as the quality of empirical intuition specifically differentiating it from other sensations, can never be known *a priori*, yet it can, in a possible experience in general, as quantity of perception be intensively distinguished from every other similar perception. Hence the application of mathematics to nature, as regards the sensuous intuition by which nature is given to us, thus becomes possible and definite.

Above all, the reader must pay attention to the mode of proof of the principles which occur under the title of "analogies of experience." For these do not refer to the genesis of intuitions, as do the principles of applying mathematics to natural science in general, but to the connection of their existence in an experience; and this can be nothing but the determination of their existence in time according to necessary laws, under which alone the connection is objectively valid and thus becomes experience. The proof, therefore, does not turn on the synthetical unity in the connection of things in themselves, but merely of perceptions; and of these, not in regard to their matter, but to the determination of time and of the relation of their existence in it according to universal laws. If the empirical determination in relative time is indeed to be objectively valid (that is, to be experience), these universal laws must contain the necessary determination of existence in time generally (namely, according to a rule of the understanding *a priori*).

As these are prolegomena I cannot here further descant on the subject, but my reader (who has probably been long accustomed to consider experience a mere empirical synthesis of perceptions, and hence has not considered that it goes much beyond them since it imparts to empirical judgments universal validity, and for that purpose requires a pure and *a priori* unity of the understanding) is recommended to pay special attention to this distinction of experience from a mere aggregate of perceptions and to judge the mode of proof from this point of view.

§ 27. Now we are prepared to remove Hume's doubt. He justly maintains that we cannot comprehend by reason the possibility of causality, that is, of the reference of the existence of one thing to the existence of another which is necessitated by the former. I add that we comprehend just as little the concept of subsistence, that is, the necessity that at the foundation of the existence of things there lies a subject which cannot itself be a predicate of any other thing; nay, we cannot even form a notion of the possibility of such a thing (though we can point out examples of its use in experience). The very same incomprehensibility affects the community of things, as we cannot comprehend how from the state of one thing an inference to the state of quite another thing beyond it, and *vice versa,* can be drawn, and how substances which have each their own separate existence should depend upon one another necessarily. But I am very far from holding these concepts to be derived merely from experience, and the necessity represented in them to be imaginary and a mere illusion produced in us by long habit. On the contrary, I have amply shown that they and the principles derived from them are firmly established *a priori* before all experience and have their undoubted objective value, though only with regard to experience.

§28. Although I have no notion of such a connection of things in themselves, how they can either exist as substances, or act as causes, or stand in community with others (as parts of a real whole), and I can just as little conceive such properties in appearances as such (because those concepts contain nothing that lies in the appearances, but only what the understanding alone must think), we have yet a concept of such a connection of representations in our understanding and in judgments generally. This concept is: that representations appear, in one sort of judgments, as subject in relation to predicates; in another, as ground in relation to consequent; and, in a third, as parts which constitute together a total possible cognition. Furthermore, we know *a priori* that without considering the representation of an object as determined in one or the other of these respects, we can have no valid knowledge of the object; and, if we should occupy ourselves about the object in itself, there is not a single possible attribute by which I could know that it is determined under any of these aspects, that is, under the concept either of substance, or of cause, or (in relation to other substances) of community, for I have no concept of the possibility of such a connection of existence. But the question is not how things in themselves but how the empirical knowledge of things is determined, as regards the above aspects of judgments in general; that is, how things, as objects of experience, can and must be subsumed under these concepts of the understanding. And then it is clear that I completely comprehend, not only the possibility, but also the necessity, of subsuming all appearances under these concepts—that is, of using them for principles of the possibility of experience.

§ 29. In order to test Hume's problematical concept (his *crux metaphysicorum*), the concept of cause, we are first given *a priori*, by means of logic, the form of a conditional judgment in general; that is, we have one cognition given as antecedent and another as consequent. But it is possible that in perception we may meet with a rule of relation which runs thus: that a certain appearance is constantly followed by another (though not conversely); and this is a case for me to use the hypothetical judgment and, for instance, to say if the sun shines long enough upon a body it grows warm. Here there is indeed as yet no necessity of connection or concept of cause. But I proceed and say that, if this proposition, which is merely a subjective connection of perceptions, is to be a proposition of experience, it must be seen as necessary and universally valid. Such a proposition would be that the sun is by its light the cause of heat. The empirical rule is now considered as a law, and as valid, not merely of appearances but valid of them for the purposes of a possible experience which requires universal and therefore necessarily valid rules. I therefore easily comprehend the concept of cause, as a concept necessarily belonging to the mere form of experience, and its possibility as a synthetical union of perceptions in consciousness in general; but I do not at all comprehend the possibility of a thing in general as a cause, because the concept of cause denotes a condition not at all belonging to things, but to experience. For experience can be nothing but objectively valid knowledge of appearances and of their succession, only so far as the earlier can be conjoined with the later according to the rule of hypothetical judgments.

§ 30. Hence if even the pure concepts of the understanding are thought to go beyond objects of experience to things in themselves (*noumena*), they have no meaning whatever. They serve, as it were, only to decipher appearances, that we may be able to read them as experience. The principles which arise from their reference to the sensible world only serve our understanding for empirical use. Beyond this they are arbitrary combinations without objective reality, and we can neither know their possibility *a priori* nor verify—or even render intelligible by any example— their reference to objects; because examples can only be borrowed from some possible experience, and consequently the objects of these concepts can be found nowhere but in a possible experience.

This complete (though to its originator unexpected) solution of Hume's problem rescues for the pure concepts of the understanding their *a priori* origin and for the universal laws of nature their validity as laws of the understanding, yet in such a way as to limit their use to experience, because their possibility depends solely on the reference of the understanding to experience, but with a completely reversed mode of connection which never occurred to Hume—they do not derive from experience, but experience derives from them.

This is, therefore, the result of all our foregoing inquiries: "All synthetical principles *a priori* are nothing more than principles of possible experience" and can never be referred to things in themselves, but to appearances as objects of experience. And hence pure mathematics as well as a pure science of nature can never be referred to anything more than mere appearances, and can only represent either that which makes experience in general possible, or else that which, as it is derived from these principles, must always be capable of being represented in some possible experience.

§ 31. And thus we have at last something definite upon which to depend in all metaphysical enterprises, which have hitherto, boldly enough but always blindly, attempted everything without discrimination. That the aim of their exertions should be so near struck neither the dogmatic thinkers nor those who, confident in their supposed sound common sense, started with concepts and principles of pure reason (which were legitimate and natural, but destined for mere empirical use) in quest of insights to which they neither knew nor could know any definite bounds, because they had never reflected nor were able to reflect on the nature or even on the possibility of such a pure understanding.

Many a naturalist of pure reason (by which I mean the man who believes he can decide in matters of metaphysics without any science) may pretend that he, long ago, by the prophetic spirit of his sound sense, not only suspected but knew and comprehended what is here propounded with so much ado, or, if he likes, with prolix and pedantic pomp: "that with all our reason we can never reach beyond the field of experience." But when he is questioned about his rational principles individually, he must grant that there are many of them which he has not taken from experience and which are therefore independent of it and valid *a priori*. How then and on what grounds will he restrain both himself and the dogmatist, who makes use of these concepts and principles beyond all possible experience because they are recognized to be independent of it? And even he, this adept in sound sense, in spite of all his assumed and cheaply acquired wisdom, is not exempt from wandering inadvertently beyond objects of experience into the field of chimeras. He is often deeply enough involved in them; though, in announcing everything as mere probability, rational conjecture, or analogy, he gives by his popular language a color to his groundless pretensions.

§ 32. Since the oldest days of philosophy, inquirers into pure reason have conceived, besides the things of sense, or appearances (*phenomena*), which make up the sensible world, certain beings of the understanding [8] (*noumena*), which should constitute an intelligible world. And as appearance and illusion were by those men identified (a thing which we may well excuse in an undeveloped epoch), actuality was only conceded to the beings of the understanding.

And we indeed, rightly considering objects of sense as mere

[8] [*Verstandeswesen.*]

appearances, confess thereby that they are based upon a thing in itself, though we know not this thing as it is in itself but only know its appearances, namely, the way in which our senses are affected by this unknown something. The understanding, therefore, by assuming appearances, grants the existence of things in themselves also; and to this extent we may say that the representation of such things as are the basis of appearances, consequently of mere beings of the understanding, is not only admissible but unavoidable.

Our critical deduction by no means excludes things of that sort (*noumena*), but rather limits the principles of the Aesthetic [9] to this, that they shall not extend to all things—as everything would then be turned into mere appearance—but that they shall hold good only of objects of possible experience. Hereby, then, beings of the understanding are granted, but with the inculcation of this rule which admits of no exception: that we neither know nor can know anything at all definite of these pure beings of the understanding, because our pure concepts of the understanding as well as our pure intuitions extend to nothing but objects of possible experience, consequently to mere things of sense; and as soon as we leave this sphere, these concepts retain no meaning whatever.

§ 33.   There is indeed something seductive in our pure concepts of the understanding which tempts us to a transcendent use—a use which transcends all possible experience. Not only are our concepts of substance, of power, of action, of reality, and others, quite independent of experience, containing nothing of sense appearance, and so apparently applicable to things in themselves (*noumena*), but, what strengthens this conjecture, they contain a necessity of determination in themselves, which experience never attains. The concept of cause implies a rule according to which one state follows another necessarily; but experience can only show us that one state of things often or, at most, commonly follows another, and therefore affords neither strict universality nor necessity.

[9] [That is, the first part of the *Critique of Pure Reason,* establishing space and time as pure intuitions.—L.W.B.]

Hence the concepts of the understanding seem to have a deeper meaning and import than can be exhausted by their merely empirical use, and so the understanding inadvertently adds for itself to the house of experience a much more extensive wing, which it fills with nothing but beings of thought, without ever observing that it has transgressed with its otherwise legitimate concepts the bounds of their use.

§ 34. Two important and even indispensable, though very dry, investigations therefore became indispensable in the *Critique of Pure Reason* [namely, the chapters "The Schematism of the Pure Concepts of the Understanding" and "On the Ground of the Distinction of All Objects as Phenomena and Noumena."] In the former it is shown that the senses furnish, not the pure concepts of the understanding *in concreto,* but only the schema for their use, and that the object conformable to it occurs only in experience (as the product of the understanding from materials of the sensibility). In the latter it is shown that, although our pure concepts of the understanding and our principles are independent of experience, and despite the apparently greater sphere of their use, still nothing whatever can be thought by them beyond the field of experience, because they can do nothing but merely determine the logical form of the judgment relatively to given intuitions. But as there is no intuition at all beyond the field of the sensibility, these pure concepts, as they cannot possibly be exhibited *in concreto,* are void of all meaning; consequently all these *noumena,* together with their complex, the intelligible world,[10] are nothing but representation of a problem, of which the object in itself is possible but the solution, from the

---

[10] We speak of the "intelligible world," not (as the usual expression is) "intellectual world." For cognitions are intellectual through the understanding and refer to our world of sense also; but objects, in so far as they can be represented merely by the understanding, and to which none of our sensible intuitions can refer, are termed "intelligible." But as some possible intuition must correspond to every object, we would have to assume an understanding that intuits things immediately; but of such we have not the least notion, nor have we any notion of the *beings of the understanding* to which it should be applied.

nature of our understanding, totally impossible. For our understanding is not a faculty of intuition, but of the connection of given intuitions in one experience. Experience must therefore contain all the objects for our concepts; but beyond it no concepts have any significance, as there is no intuition that might offer them a foundation.

§ 35. The imagination may perhaps be forgiven for occasional vagaries and for not keeping carefully within the limits of experience, since it gains life and vigor by such flights and since it is always easier to moderate its boldness than to stimulate its languor. But the understanding which ought to *think* can never be forgiven for indulging in vagaries; for we depend upon it alone for assistance to set bounds, when necessary, to the vagaries of the imagination.

But the understanding begins its aberrations very innocently and modestly. It first brings to light the elementary cognitions which inhere in it prior to all experience, but which yet must always have their application in experience. It gradually drops these limits—and what is there to prevent it, as it has quite freely derived its principles from itself? It then proceeds first to newly imagined powers in nature, then to beings outside nature— in short, to a world for whose construction the materials cannot be wanting, because fertile fiction furnishes them abundantly, and though not confirmed it is never refuted by experience. This is the reason that young thinkers are so partial to metaphysics constructed in a truly dogmatic manner, and often sacrifice to it their time and their talents, which might be otherwise better employed.

But there is no use in trying to moderate these fruitless endeavors of pure reason by all manner of cautions as to the difficulties of solving questions so occult, by complaints of the limits of our reason, and by degrading our assertions into mere conjectures. For if their impossibility is not distinctly shown, and reason's knowledge of itself does not become a true science, in which the field of its right use is distinguished, so to say, with geometrical certainty from that of its worthless and idle use, these fruitless efforts will never be wholly abandoned.

§ 36. How is nature itself possible? This question—the highest point that transcendental philosophy can ever reach, and to which, as its boundary and completion, it must proceed—really contains two questions.

First: How is nature in the material sense, that is, as to intuition, or considered as the totality of appearances, possible; how are space, time, and that which fills both—the object of sensation—possible generally? The answer is: By means of the constitution of our sensibility, according to which it is in its own way affected by objects which are in themselves unknown to it and totally distinct from those appearances. This answer is given in the *Critique* itself in the "Transcendental Aesthetic," and in these *Prolegomena* by the solution of the first general problem.

Secondly: How is nature possible in the formal sense, as the totality of the rules under which all appearances must come in order to be thought as connected in experience? The answer must be this: It is only possible by means of the constitution of our understanding, according to which all the above representations of the sensibility are necessarily referred to a consciousness, and by which the peculiar way in which we think (namely, by rules) and hence experience also are possible, but must be clearly distinguished from an insight into the objects in themselves. This answer is given in the *Critique* itself in the "Transcendental Logic" and in these *Prolegomena,* in the course of the solution of the second main problem.

But how this peculiar property of our sensibility itself is possible, or that of our understanding and of the apperception which is necessarily its basis and that of all thinking, cannot be further analyzed or answered, because it is of them that we are in need for all our answers and for all our thinking about objects.

There are many laws of nature which we can know only by means of experience; but conformity to law in the connection of appearances, that is, in nature in general, we cannot discover by any experience, because experience itself requires laws which are *a priori* at the basis of its possibility.

The possibility of experience in general is therefore at the same time the universal law of nature, and the principles of experience are the very laws of nature. For we know nature only as the totality of appearances, that is, of representations in us; and hence we can only derive the laws of their connection from the principles of their connection in us, that is, from the conditions of their necessary union in one consciousness which constitutes the possibility of experience.

Even the main proposition expounded throughout this section —that universal laws of nature can be known *a priori*—leads naturally to the proposition that the highest legislation of nature must lie in ourselves, that is, in our understanding; and that we must not seek the universal laws of nature in nature by means of experience, but conversely must seek nature, as to its universal conformity to law, in the conditions of the possibility of experience which lie in our sensibility and in our understanding. For how were it otherwise possible to know *a priori* these laws, as they are not rules of analytical knowledge but truly synthetical extensions of it?

Such a necessary agreement of the principles of possible experience with the laws of the possibility of nature can only proceed from one of two causes: either these laws are drawn from nature by means of experience, or conversely nature is derived from the laws of the possibility of experience in general and is quite the same as the mere universal conformity to law of the latter. The former is self-contradictory, for the universal laws of nature can and must be known *a priori* (that is, independently of all experience) and be the foundation of all empirical use of the understanding; the latter alternative therefore alone remains.[11]

But we must distinguish the empirical laws of nature, which always presuppose particular perceptions, from the pure or universal laws of nature, which, without being based on particular

[11] Crusius alone thought of a compromise: that a spirit, who can neither err nor deceive, implanted these laws in us originally. But since false principles often intrude themselves, as indeed the very system of this man shows in not a few instances, we are involved in difficulties as to the use of such a principle in the absence of sure criteria to distinguish the genuine origin from the spurious, since we never can know certainly what the spirit of truth or the father of lies may have instilled into us.

perceptions, contain merely the conditions of their necessary union in experience. In relation to the latter, nature and possible experience are quite the same; and as the conformity to law in the latter depends upon the necessary connection of appearances in experience (without which we cannot know any object whatever in the sensible world), consequently upon the original laws of the understanding, it seems at first strange, but is not the less certain, to say: *The understanding does not derive its laws* (a priori) *from, but prescribes them to, nature.*

§ 37. We shall illustrate this seemingly bold proposition by an example, which will show that laws which we discover in objects of sensuous intuition (especially when these laws are known as necessary) are commonly held by us to be such as have been placed there by the understanding, in spite of their being similar in all points to the laws of nature which we ascribe to experience.

§ 38. If we consider the properties of the circle, by which this figure combines in itself so many arbitrary determinations of space in a universal rule, we cannot avoid attributing a constitution [12] to this geometrical thing. Two straight lines, for example, which intersect each other and the circle, howsoever they may be drawn, are always divided so that the rectangle constructed with the segments of the one is equal to that constructed with the segments of the other. The question now is: Does this law lie in the circle or in the understanding? That is, does this figure, independently of the understanding, contain in itself the ground of the law; or does the understanding, having constructed according to its concepts (of the equality of the radii) the figure itself, introduce into it this law of the chords intersecting in geometrical proportion? When we follow the proofs of this law, we soon perceive that it can only be derived from the condition on which the understanding founds the construction of this figure, namely, the concept of the equality of the radii. But if we enlarge this concept to pursue further the unity of various properties of geometrical figures under common laws and consider the

[12] [*Eine Natur.*]

circle as a conic section, which of course is subject to the same fundamental conditions of construction as other conic sections, we shall find that all the chords which intersect within the ellipse, parabola, and hyperbola always intersect so that the rectangles of their segments are not indeed equal but always bear a constant ratio to one another. If we proceed still farther to the fundamental teachings of physical astronomy, we find a physical law of reciprocal attraction applicable to all material nature, the rule of which is that it decreases inversely as the square of the distance from each attracting point, that is, as the spherical surfaces increase over which this force spreads, which law seems to be necessarily inherent in the very nature of things, and hence is usually propounded as knowable *a priori*. Simple as the sources of this law are, merely resting upon the relation of spherical surfaces of different radii, its consequences are so valuable with regard to the variety and simplicity of their agreement that not only are all possible orbits of the celestial bodies conic sections, but such a relation of these orbits to one another results that no other law of attraction than that of the inverse square of the distance can be imagined as fit for a cosmical system.

Here accordingly is nature, which rests upon laws that the understanding knows *a priori*, and chiefly from the universal principles of the determination of space. Now I ask: Do the laws of nature lie in space, and does the understanding learn them by merely endeavoring to find out the enormous wealth of meaning that lies in space; or do they inhere in the understanding and in the way in which it determines space according to the conditions of the synthetical unity in which its concepts are all centered?

Space is something so uniform and as to all particular properties so indeterminate that we should certainly not seek a store of laws of nature in it. Whereas that which determines space to assume the form of a circle, or the figures of a cone and a sphere, is the understanding, so far as it contains the ground of the unity of their constructions.

The mere universal form of intuition, called space, must therefore be the substratum of all intuitions determinable to particular objects; and in it, of course, the condition of the possibility and of the variety of these intuitions lies. But the unity of the objects is entirely determined by the understanding and on conditions which lie in its own nature; and thus the understanding is the origin of the universal order of nature, in that it comprehends all appearances under its own laws and thereby produces, in an *a priori* manner, experience (as to its form), by means of which whatever is to be known only by experience is necessarily subjected to its laws. For we are not concerned with the nature of things in themselves, which is independent of the conditions both of our sensibility and our understanding, but with nature as an object of possible experience; and in this case the understanding, since it makes experience possible, thereby insists that the sensuous world is either not an object of experience at all or that it is nature [namely, the existence of things determined according to universal laws].[13]

§ 39

APPENDIX TO THE PURE SCIENCE OF NATURE

Of the System of the Categories

There can be nothing more desirable to a philosopher than to be able to derive the scattered multiplicity of the concepts or principles which had occurred to him in concrete use from a principle *a priori,* and to unite everything in this way in one cognition. He formerly only believed that those things which remained after a certain abstraction, and seemed by comparison among one another to constitute a particular kind of cognitions, were completely collected; but this was only an *aggregate.* Now

[13] [Cf. § 14, beginning.—Carus.]

he knows that just so many, neither more nor less, can constitute the kind of cognition, and perceives the necessity of his division. This constitutes comprehension; and only then has he attained a *system*.

To search in our common knowledge for the concepts which do not rest upon particular experience and yet occur in all knowledge from experience, of which they as it were constitute the mere form of connection, presupposes neither greater reflection nor deeper insight than to detect in a language the rules of the actual use of words generally and thus to collect elements for a grammar (in fact both researches are very nearly related), even though we are not able to give a reason why each language has just this and no other formal constitution, and still less why any precise number of such formal determinations in general, neither more nor less, can be found in it.

Aristotle collected ten pure elementary concepts under the name of *categories*.[14] To these, which are also called "predicaments," he found himself obliged afterward to add five post-predicaments,[15] some of which however (*prius, simul,* and *motus*) are contained in the former; but this rhapsody must be considered (and commended) as a mere hint for future inquirers, not as an idea developed according to rule; and hence it has, in the present more advanced state of philosophy, been rejected as quite useless.

After long reflection on the pure elements of human knowledge (those which contain nothing empirical), I at last succeeded in distinguishing with certainty and in separating the pure elementary notions of the sensibility (space and time) from those of the understanding. Thus the seventh, eighth, and ninth categories had to be excluded from the old list. And the others were of no service to me because there was no principle on which the understanding could be exhaustively investigated, and all the functions, whence its pure concepts arise, determined exhaustively and precisely.

[14] 1. *Substantia.* 2. *Qualitas.* 3. *Quantitas.* 4. *Relatio.* 5. *Actio.* 6. *Passio.* 7. *Quando.* 8. *Ubi.* 9. *Situs.* 10. *Habitus.*
[15] *Oppositum. Prius. Simul. Motus. Habere.*

But in order to discover such a principle, I looked about for an act of the understanding which comprises all the rest and is distinguished only by various modifications or phases, in reducing the multiplicity of representation to the unity of thinking in general. I found this act of the understanding to consist in judging. Here, then, the labors of the logicians were ready at hand, though not yet quite free from defects; and with this help I was enabled to exhibit a complete table of the pure functions of the understanding, which are however undetermined with respect to any object. I finally referred these functions of judging to objects in general, or rather to the condition of determining judgments as objectively valid; and so there arose the pure concepts of the understanding, concerning which I could make certain that these, and this exact number only, constitute our whole knowledge of things by pure understanding. I was justified in calling them by their old name "categories," while I reserved for myself the liberty of adding, under the title of "predicables," a complete list of all the concepts deducible from them by combinations, whether among themselves, or with the pure form of the appearance, that is, space or time, or with its matter, so far as it is not yet empirically determined (namely, the object of sensation in .general), as soon as a system of transcendental philosophy should be completed, with the construction of which I was engaged in the *Critique of Pure Reason* itself.

Now the essential point in this system of categories, which distinguishes it from the old rhapsody which proceeded without any principle and for which alone it deserves to be considered as philosophy, consists in this: that, by means of it, the true significance of the pure concepts of the understanding and the condition of their use could be precisely determined. For here it became obvious that they are themselves nothing but logical functions, and as such do not produce the least concept of an object, but require sensuous intuition as a basis. These concepts, therefore, only serve to determine empirical judgments (which are otherwise undetermined and indifferent as regards all functions of judging) with respect to the functions of judging, thereby procuring them universal validity and, by means of them, making judgments of experience in general possible.

Such an insight into the nature of the categories, which limits them at the same time to use merely in experience, never occurred either to their first author or to any of his successors; but without this insight (which immediately depends upon their derivation or deduction), they are quite useless and only a miserable list of names, without explanation or rule for their use. Had the ancients ever conceived such a notion, doubtless the whole study of pure rational knowledge, which under the name of metaphysics has for centuries spoiled many a sound mind, would have reached us in quite another shape and would have enlightened the human understanding, instead of actually exhausting it in obscure and vain speculations and rendering it unfit for true science.

This system of categories makes all treatment of every object of pure reason itself systematic, and affords a direction or clue how and through what points of inquiry every metaphysical consideration must proceed in order to be complete; for it exhausts all the possible functions [16] of the understanding, among which every concept must be classed. In like manner the table of principles has been formulated, the completeness of which we can only vouch for by the system of the categories. Even in the division of the concepts,[17] which must go beyond the physical application of the understanding, it is always the very same clue, which, as it must always be determined *a priori* by the same fixed points of the human understanding, always forms a closed circle. There is no doubt that the object of a pure concept, either of the understanding or of reason, so far as it is to be estimated philosophically and on *a priori* principles, can in this way be completely known. I could not therefore omit to make use of this clue with regard to one of the most abstract ontological divisions, namely, the various distinctions of the concepts of something

[16] [*Momente.*]

[17] *Cf.* the tables in the *Critique of Pure Reason* in the chapters on "The Paralogisms of Pure Reason" and the "System of Cosmological Ideas."

and of nothing, and to construct accordingly [18] a systematic and necessary table of their divisions.[19]

And this system, like every other true one founded on a universal principle, shows its inestimable value in that it excludes all foreign concepts which might otherwise intrude among the pure concepts of the understanding, and determines the place of every cognition. Those concepts, which under the name of "concepts of reflection" have been likewise arranged in a table according to the clue of the categories, intrude into ontology without any privilege or just claim to be among the pure concepts of the understanding. The latter are concepts of connection, and thereby of the objects themselves, whereas the former are only concepts of mere comparison of concepts already given, and hence are of quite another nature and use. By my systematic division [20] they are saved from this confusion. But the value of the special table of the categories will be still more obvious when we separate—

[18] In the chapter on "The Amphiboly of the Concepts of Reflection," in the *Critique of Pure Reason*.

[19] On the table of the categories many neat observations may be made, for instance: (1) that the third arises from the first and the second, joined in one concept; (2) that in those of quantity and of quality there is merely a progress from unity to totality or from something to nothing (for this purpose the categories of quality must stand thus: reality, limitation, total negation), without *correlata* or *opposita*, whereas those of relation and of modality have them; (3) that, as in logic categorical judgments are the basis of all others, so the category of substance is the basis of all concepts of actual things; (4) that, as modality in the judgment is not a particular predicate, so by the modal concepts a determination is not superadded to things, etc. Such observations are of great use. If we enumerate all the predicables, which we can find pretty completely in any good ontology (for example, Baumgarten's), and arrange them in classes under the categories, in which operation we must not neglect to add as complete a dissection of all these concepts as possible, there will then arise a merely analytical part of metaphysics which does not contain a single synthetical proposition, which might precede the second (the synthetical) and would, by its precision and completeness, be not only useful but, in virtue of its system, be even to some extent elegant.

[20] See *Critique of Pure Reason*, "The Amphiboly of the Concepts of Reflection."

as we are about to do—the table of the transcendental concepts of reason from the concepts of the understanding. As the transcendental concepts of reason are of an entirely different nature and origin, the table of them must have quite another form than the table of categories. This so necessary separation has never yet been made in any system of metaphysics, where, as a rule, these Ideas of reason are all mixed up with the concepts of the understanding, as if they were children of the same family—a confusion which was unavoidable in the absence of a definite system of categories.

THIRD PART OF THE MAIN TRANSCEN-
DENTAL PROBLEM

HOW IS METAPHYSICS IN GENERAL POSSIBLE?

§ 40

PURE mathematics and pure science of nature had, for their own safety and certainty, no need for such a deduction as we have made of both. For the former rests upon its own evidence, and the latter (though sprung from pure sources of the understanding) upon experience and its thorough confirmation. The pure science of nature cannot altogether refuse and dispense with the testimony of experience; because with all its certainty it can never, as philosophy, rival mathematics. Both sciences, therefore, stood in need of this inquiry, not for themselves, but for the sake of another science: metaphysics.

Metaphysics has to do not only with concepts of nature, which always find their application in experience, but also with pure rational concepts, which never can be given in any possible experience whatever. Consequently it deals with concepts whose objective reality (namely, that they are not mere chimeras) and with assertions whose truth or falsity cannot be discovered or confirmed by any experience. This part of metaphysics, however, is precisely what constitutes its essential end, to which the rest is only a means, and thus this science is in need of such a deduction for its own sake. The third question now proposed relates therefore as it were to the root and peculiarity of metaphysics, that is, the occupation of reason merely with itself and the supposed knowledge of objects arising immediately from this brooding over its own concepts, without requiring, or indeed being able to reach that knowledge through, experience.[1]

Without solving this problem, reason can never satisfy itself. The empirical use to which reason limits the pure understanding does not fully satisfy the proper calling of reason. Every single experience is only a part of the whole sphere of its domain, but the absolute totality of all possible experience is itself not experience. Yet it is a necessary problem for reason, the mere representation of which requires concepts quite different from the pure concepts of the understanding, whose use is only *immanent*, or refers to experience, so far as it can be given. Whereas the concepts of reason aim at the completeness, that is, the collective unity of all possible experience, and thereby transcend every given experience. Thus they become *transcendent*.

As the understanding stands in need of categories for experience, reason contains in itself the source of Ideas, by which I mean necessary concepts whose object *cannot* be given in any experience. The latter are inherent in the nature of reason, as the former are in that of the understanding. While the former carry with them an illusion likely to mislead, the illusion of the latter is inevitable, though it certainly can be kept from misleading us.

Since all illusion consists in holding the subjective ground of our judgments to be objective, a self-knowledge of pure reason in its transcendent (presumptuous) use is the sole preservative from the aberrations into which reason falls when it mistakes its calling and transcendently refers to the object that which concerns only its own subject and its guidance in all immanent use.

§ 41. The distinction of Ideas—that is, of pure concepts of reason—from categories, or pure concepts of the understanding, as cognitions of a quite distinct species, origin, and use, is so

[1] If we can say that a science is actual, at least in the idea of all men, as soon as it appears that the problems which lead to it are proposed to everybody by the nature of human reason, and that therefore many (though faulty) endeavors are unavoidably made in its behalf, then we are bound to say that metaphysics is subjectively (and indeed necessarily) actual, and therefore, we justly ask, how is it (objectively) possible.

important a point in founding a science which is to contain the system of all these *a priori* cognitions that, without this distinction, metaphysics is absolutely impossible or is at best a random, bungling attempt to build a castle in the air without a knowledge of the materials or of their fitness for this or any purpose. Had the *Critique of Pure Reason* done nothing but first point out this distinction, it would thereby have contributed more to clear up our conception of, and to guide our inquiry in, the field of metaphysics than all the vain efforts which had hitherto been made to satisfy the transcendent problems of pure reason, but which had never surmised that we were in quite another field than that of the understanding, and hence classed concepts of the understanding and those of reason together as if they were of the same kind.

§ 42. All pure cognitions of the understanding have this feature that their concepts present themselves in experience, and their principles can be confirmed by it; whereas the transcendent cognitions of reason cannot either, as Ideas, appear in experience or, as propositions, ever be confirmed or refuted by it. Hence whatever errors may slip in unawares can only be discovered by pure reason itself—a discovery of much difficulty, because this very reason naturally becomes dialectical by means of its Ideas; and this unavoidable illusion cannot be limited by any objective and dogmatic researches into things, but only by a subjective investigation of reason itself as a source of ideas.

§ 43. In the *Critique of Pure Reason* it was always my greatest care to endeavor, not only carefully to distinguish the several species of knowledge, but to derive concepts belonging to each one of them from their common source. I did this in order that, by knowing whence they originated, I might determine their use with safety and also have the unanticipated but invaluable advantage of knowing, according to principles, the completeness of my enumeration, classification, and specification of concepts *a priori*. Without this, metaphysics is mere rhapsody, in which no one knows whether he has enough or whether and where something is still wanting. We can indeed have this advantage only in pure philosophy, but of this philosophy it constitutes the very essence.

As I had found the origin of the categories in the four logical forms of all the judgments of the understanding, it was quite natural to seek the origin of the Ideas in the three forms of syllogisms. For as soon as these pure concepts of reason (the transcendental Ideas) are given, they could hardly, except they be held innate, be found anywhere else than in the same activity of reason, which, so far as it regards mere form, constitutes the logical element of syllogisms; but, so far as it represents judgments of the understanding as determined *a priori* with respect to one or another form, constitutes transcendental concepts of pure reason.

The formal distinction of syllogisms renders necessary their division into categorical, hypothetical, and disjunctive. The concepts of reason founded on them contain therefore, first, the Idea of the complete subject (the substantial); secondly, the Idea of the complete series of conditions; thirdly, the determination of all concepts in the Idea of a complete complex of that which is possible.[2] The first idea is psychological, the second cosmological, the third theological; and, as all three give occasion to dialectic, yet each in its own way, the division of the whole dialectic of pure reason into its paralogism, its antinomy, and its Ideal was arranged accordingly. Through this deduction we may feel assured that all the claims of pure reason are completely

---

[2] In disjunctive judgments, we consider all possibility as divided in respect to a particular concept. By the ontological principle of the universal determination of a thing in general, I understand the principle that either the one or the other of all possible contradictory predicates must be assigned to any object. This is, at the same time, the principle of all disjunctive judgments, constituting the foundation of a complete whole of possibility, and in it the possibility of every object in general is considered as determined. This may serve as a slight explanation of the above propositions: that the activity of reason in disjunctive syllogisms is formally the same as that by which it fashions the idea of a complete whole of all reality, containing in itself that which is positive in all pairs of contradictory predicates.

represented and that none can be wanting, because the faculty of reason itself, whence they all take their origin, is thereby completely surveyed.

§ 44. In these general considerations it is also remarkable that the Ideas of reason, unlike the categories, are of no service to the use of our understanding in experience, but quite dispensable, and become even an impediment to the maxims of a rational knowledge of nature. Yet in another aspect still to be determined they are necessary. Whether the soul is or is not a simple substance is of no consequence to us in the explanation of its phenomena. For we cannot render the concept of a simple being sensuous and thus concretely intelligible by any possible experience. The concept is therefore quite void as regards all hoped-for insight into the cause of appearances and cannot at all serve as a principle of the explanation of that which inner or outer experience supplies. Similarly, the cosmological Ideas of the beginning of the world or of its eternity (*a parte ante*) cannot be of any service to us for the explanation of any event in the world itself. And finally we must, according to a right maxim of the philosophy of nature, refrain from explaining the design of nature as drawn from the will of a Supreme Being, because this would not be natural philosophy but a confession that we have come to the end of it. The use of these Ideas, therefore, is quite different from that of those categories by which (and by the principles built upon which) experience itself first becomes possible. But our laborious Analytic of the understanding would be superfluous if we had nothing else in view than the mere knowledge of nature as it can be given in experience; for reason does its work, both in mathematics and in the science of nature, quite safely and well without any of this subtle deduction. Therefore our critical examination of the understanding combines with the Ideas of pure reason for a purpose which lies beyond the empirical use of the understanding; but such an extended use of the understanding we have above declared to be totally inadmissible and without any object or meaning. Yet there must be a harmony between the nature of reason and that of the understanding, and the former must contribute to the perfection of the latter and cannot possibly upset it.

The solution of this question is as follows: Pure reason does not in its Ideas point to particular objects which lie beyond the field of experience, but only requires completeness of the use of the understanding in the system of experience. But this completeness can be a completeness of principles only, not of intuitions and of objects. In order, however, to represent the Ideas definitely, reason conceives them after the fashion of the knowledge of an object. This knowledge is, as far as these rules are concerned, completely determined; but the object is only an Idea [invented for the purpose of] bringing the knowledge of the understanding as near as possible to the completeness indicated by that Idea.

PREFATORY REMARK TO THE DIALECTIC OF PURE REASON

§ 45. We have shown in §§ 33 and 34 that the purity of the categories from all admixture of sensuous restrictions [3] may mislead reason into extending their use beyond all experience to things in themselves; for though these categories themselves find no intuition which can give them meaning or sense *in concreto,* they, as mere logical functions, can represent a thing in general, but not give by themselves alone a determinate concept of anything. Such hyperbolical objects are distinguished by the appellation of *noumena,* or pure beings of the understanding (or better, beings of thought)—such as, for example, "substance"—but conceived without permanence in time, or "cause," but not acting in time, etc. Here predicates that only serve to make the conformity-to-law of experience possible are applied to these concepts, and yet they are deprived of all the conditions of intuition on which alone experience is possible, and so these concepts lose all significance.

There is no danger, however, of the understanding spontaneously making an excursion so very wantonly beyond its own

[3] [*Bestimmungen.*]

bounds into the field of the mere beings of thought unless it is impelled by foreign laws. But when reason, which cannot be fully satisfied with any empirical use of the rules of the understanding, as being always conditioned, requires a completion of this chain of conditions, then the understanding is forced out of its sphere. And then it partly represents objects of experience in a series so extended that no experience can grasp it; partly even (with a view to complete the series) it seeks entirely beyond it *noumena*, to which it can attach that chain; and so, having at last escaped from the conditions of experience, it makes its stand as it were final. These are then the transcendental Ideas, which, in accord with the true but hidden ends of the natural destiny of our reason, aim, not at extravagant concepts, but at an unbounded extension of their empirical use, yet seduce the understanding by an unavoidable illusion to a transcendent use, which, though deceitful, cannot be restrained within the bounds of experience by any resolution, but only by scientific instruction and with much difficulty.

I. THE PSYCHOLOGICAL IDEAS [4]

§ 46.   People have long since observed that in all substances the subject proper, that which remains after all the accidents (as predicates) are abstracted, consequently the *substantial*, remains unknown, and various complaints have been made concerning these limits to our knowledge. But it will be well to consider that the human understanding is not to be blamed for its inability to know the substance of things—that is, to determine it by itself—but rather for demanding definitely to know substance, which is a mere Idea, as though it were a given object. Pure reason requires us to seek for every predicate of a thing its own subject, and for this subject, which is itself necessarily nothing but a predicate, its subject, and so on indefinitely (or as far as we can reach). But hence it follows that we must not hold anything at which we can arrive to be an ultimate subject,

[4] See *Critique of Pure Reason*, "The Paralogisms of Pure Reason."

and that substance itself never can be thought by our understanding, however deep we may penetrate, even if all nature were
unveiled to us. For the specific nature of our understanding consists in thinking everything discursively, that is, by concepts,
and so by mere predicates, to which, therefore, the absolute subject must always be wanting. Hence all the real properties by
which we know bodies are mere accidents—not excepting even
impenetrability, which we can only represent to ourselves as the
effect of a power of which the subject is unknown to us.

Now we appear to have this substance in the consciousness of
ourselves (in the thinking subject), and indeed in an immediate
intuition; for all the predicates of an internal sense refer to the
ego, as a subject, and I cannot conceive myself as the predicate
of any other subject. Hence completeness in the reference of the
given concepts as predicates to a subject—not merely an Idea,
but an object—that is, the absolute subject itself, seems to be
given in experience. But this expectation is disappointed. For
the ego is not a concept,[5] but only the indication of the object
of the inner sense, so far as we know it by no further predicate.
Consequently it cannot indeed be itself a predicate of any other
thing; but just as little can it be a definite concept of an absolute subject, but is, as in all other cases, only the reference of the
inner phenomena [6] to their unknown subject. Yet this idea (which
serves very well as a regulative principle totally to destroy all
materialistic explanations of the internal phenomena of the soul)
occasions by a very natural misunderstanding a very specious
argument, which infers its nature from this supposed knowledge
of the substance of our thinking being. This is specious so far as
the knowledge of it falls quite without the complex of experience.

§ 47. But though we may call this thinking self (the soul)
"substance," as being the ultimate subject of thinking which

[5] Were the representation of the apperception (the Ego) a concept,
by which anything whatever could be thought, it could be used as a
predicate of other things or contain predicates in itself. But it is nothing more than the feeling of an existence without the least concept
and is only the representation of that to which all thinking stands
in relation (*relatione accidentis*).

[6] [*Erscheinungen.*]

cannot be further represented as the predicate of another thing, it remains quite empty and without significance if permanence—the quality which renders the concept of substances in experience fruitful—cannot be proved of it.

But permanence can never be proved of the concept of a substance as a thing in itself, but for the purposes of experience only. This is sufficiently shown by the first Analogy of Experience,[7] and whoever will not yield to this proof may try for himself whether he can succeed in proving, from the concept of a subject which does not exist itself as the predicate of another thing, that its existence is absolutely permanent and that it cannot either in itself or by any natural cause originate or be annihilated. These synthetical *a priori* propositions can never be proved in themselves, but only in reference to things as objects of possible experience.

§ 48. If, therefore, from the concept of the soul as a substance we would infer its permanence, this can hold good as regards possible experience only, not of the soul as a thing in itself and beyond all possible experience. Life is the subjective condition of all our possible experience; consequently we can only infer the permanence of the soul in life, for the death of a man is the end of all experience which concerns the soul as an object of experience, except the contrary be proved—which is the very question in hand. The permanence of the soul can therefore only be proved (and no one cares to do that) during the life of man, but not, as we desire to do, after death. The reason for this is that the concept of substance, so far as it is to be considered necessarily combined with the concept of permanence, can be so combined only according to the principles of possible experience, and therefore for the purposes of experience only.[8]

---

[7] In the *Critique of Pure Reason.*

[8] It is indeed very remarkable how carelessly metaphysicians have always passed over the principle of the permanence of substances without ever attempting a proof of it; doubtless because they found themselves abandoned by all proofs as soon as they began to deal with the concept of substance. Common sense, which felt distinctly that without this presupposition no union of perceptions in experience is pos-

§ 49. That there is something real outside us which not only corresponds but must correspond to our outer perceptions can likewise be proved to be, not a connection of things in themselves, but for the sake of experience. This means that there is something empirical, that is, some appearance in space without us, that admits of a satisfactory proof; for we have nothing to do with other objects than those which belong to possible experience, because objects which cannot be given us in any experience are nothing for us. Empirically outside me is that which is intuited in space; and space, together with all the appearances it contains, belongs to the representations whose connection, according to laws of experience, proves their objective truth, just as tne connection of the appearances of the inner sense proves the actuality of my soul (as an object of the inner sense). By means of outer experience I am conscious of the actuality of bodies as external appearances in space, in the same manner as by means of the inner experience I am conscious of the existence of my soul in time; but this soul is known only as an object of the inner sense by appearances that constitute an inner state and of which the being in itself, which forms the basis of these appearances, is unknown. Cartesian idealism therefore does nothing but distinguish outer experience from a dream and the con-

sible, supplied the want by a postulate. From experience itself it never could derive such a principle, partly because material things (substances) cannot be so traced in all their alterations and dissolutions that the matter can always be found undiminished, partly because the principle contains *necessity,* which is always the sign of an *a priori* principle. People then boldly applied this postulate to the concept of soul as a *substance,* and concluded a necessary continuance of the soul after the death of man (especially as the simplicity of this substance, which is inferred from the indivisibility of consciousness, secured it from destruction by dissolution). Had they found the genuine source of this principle—a discovery which requires deeper researches than they were ever inclined to make—they would have seen that the law of the permanence of substances arises for the purposes of experience only, and hence can hold good of things so far as they are to be known and conjoined with others in experience, but never independently of all possible experience, and consequently cannot hold good of the soul after death.

formity to law (as a criterion of its truth) of the former from the irregularity and false illusion of the latter. In both it presupposes space and time as conditions of the existence of objects, and it only inquires whether the objects of the outer senses which we, when awake, put in space, are as actually to be found in it as the object of the internal sense, the soul, is in time; that is, whether experience carries with it sure criteria to distinguish it from imagination. This doubt, however, may easily be disposed of, and we always do so in common life by investigating the connection of appearances in both space and time according to universal laws of experience, and we cannot doubt, when the representation of external things throughout agrees therewith that they constitute truthful experience. Material idealism, in which appearances are considered as such only according to their connection in experience may accordingly be very easily refuted; and it is just as sure an experience that bodies exist outside us (in space) as that I myself exist according to the representation of the inner sense (in time), for the concept "outside us" only signifies existence in space. However, as the Ego in the proposition "I am" means not only the object of inner intuition (in time) but the subject of consciousness, just as body means not only outer intuition (in space) but the thing in itself which is the basis of this appearance, then the question whether bodies (as appearances of the outer sense) exist as bodies in nature apart from my thoughts may without any hesitation be denied. But the question whether I myself as an appearance of the inner sense (the soul according to empirical psychology) exist apart from my faculty of representation in time is an exactly similar one and must likewise be answered in the negative. And in this manner everything, when it is reduced to its true meaning, is decided and certain. The formal (which I have also called "transcendental") actually abolishes the material, or Cartesian, idealism. For if space be nothing but a form of my sensibility, it is as a representation in me just as actual as I myself am, and nothing but the empirical truth of the appearances in it remains for consideration. But if this is not the case, if space and the appearances in its are something existing outside us, then all the criteria of experience besides our perception can never prove the actuality of these objects outside us.

II. The Cosmological Ideas [9]

§ 50. This product of pure reason in its transcendent use is its most remarkable phenomenon. It serves as a very powerful agent to rouse philosophy from its dogmatic slumber and to stimulate it to the arduous task of undertaking a critical examination of reason itself.

I term this Idea cosmological because it always takes its object only in the sensible world and does not need any other world than one whose object is given to sense; consequently it remains in this respect in its native home, does not become transcendent, and is therefore so far not an Idea; whereas to conceive the soul as a simple substance, on the contrary, means to conceive such an object (the simple) as cannot be presented to the senses. Yet, in spite of this, the cosmological idea extends the connection of the conditioned with its condition (whether this is mathematical or dynamical) so far that experience never can keep up with it. It is therefore with regard to this point always an Idea, whose object never can be adequately given in any experience.

§ 51. In the first place, the use of a system of categories becomes here so obvious and unmistakable that, even if there were not several other proofs of it, this alone would sufficiently prove it indispensable in the system of pure reason. There are only four such transcendent Ideas, as many as there are classes of categories; in each of which, however, they refer only to the absolute completeness of the series of the conditions for a given conditioned. In accordance with these cosmological Ideas, there are only four kinds of dialectical assertions of pure reason, which, being dialectical, prove that to each of them, on equally specious principles of pure reason, a contradictory assertion stands opposed. As all the metaphysical art of the most subtle distinction cannot prevent this opposition, it compels the philosopher to

[9] Cf. *Critique of Pure Reason*, "The Antinomy of Pure Reason."

recur to the first sources of pure reason itself. This antinomy, not arbitrarily invented but founded in the nature of human reason, and hence unavoidable and never ceasing, contains the following four theses together with their antitheses:

I

Thesis: The world has, as to time and space, a beginning (limit).

Antithesis: The world is, as to time and space, infinite.

2

Thesis: Everything in the world consists of [elements that are] simple.

Antithesis: There is nothing simple, but everything is composite.

3

Thesis: There are in the world causes through freedom.

Antithesis: There is no freedom, but all is nature.

4

Thesis: In the series of the world-causes there is some necessary being.

Antithesis: There is nothing necessary in the world, but in this series all is contingent.

§52a. Here is the most singular phenomenon of human reason, no other instance of which can be shown in any other use of reason. If we, as is commonly done, represent to ourselves the appearances of the sensible world as things in themselves, if we assume the principles of their combination as principles universally valid of things in themselves and not merely of experience, as is usually, nay, without our *Critique* unavoidably, done, there arises an unexpected conflict which never can be removed in the common dogmatic way; because the thesis, as well as the antithesis, can be shown by equally clear, evident, and irresistible proofs—for I pledge myself as to the correctness of all these proofs—and reason therefore perceives that it is divided against itself, a state at which the skeptic rejoices, but which must make the critical philosopher pause and feel ill at ease.

§ 52*b*. We may blunder in various ways in metaphysics without any fear of being detected in falsehood. If we but avoid self-contradiction, which in synthetical though purely fictitious propositions is quite possible, then whenever the concepts which we connect are mere Ideas that cannot be given (with respect to their whole content) in experience, we cannot be refuted by experience. For how can we make out by experience whether the world is from eternity or had a beginning, whether matter is infinitely divisible or consists of simple parts? Such concepts cannot be given in any experience, however extensive, and consequently the falsehood either of the affirmative or the negative proposition cannot be discovered by this touchstone.

The only possible way in which reason could have revealed unintentionally its secret dialectic, falsely announced as its dogmatics, would be when it were made to ground an assertion upon a universally admitted principle and to deduce the exact contrary with the greatest accuracy of inference from another which is equally granted. This is actually here the case with regard to four natural Ideas of reason, whence four assertions on the one side and as many counterassertions on the other arise, each consistently following from universally acknowledged principles. Thus they reveal, by the use of these principles, the dialectical illusion of pure reason, which would otherwise forever remain concealed.

This is therefore a decisive experiment, which must necessarily expose any error lying hidden in the assumptions of reason.[10]

---

[10] I therefore would be pleased to have the critical reader to devote to this antinomy of pure reason his chief attention, because nature itself seems to have established it with a view to stagger reason in its daring pretensions and to force it to self-examination. For every proof which I have given of both thesis and antithesis I undertake to be responsible, and thereby to show the certainty of the inevitable antinomy of reason. When the reader is brought by this curious phenomenon to fall back upon the proof of the presumption upon which it rests, he will feel himself obliged to investigate the ultimate foundation of all knowledge by pure reason with me more thoroughly.

Contradictory propositions cannot both be false, except the concept on which each is founded is self-contradictory; for example, the propositions, "A square circle is round," and "A square circle is not round," are both false. For, as to the former, it is false that the circle is round because it is quadrangular; and it is likewise false that it is not round, that is, angular, because it is a circle. For the logical criterion of the impossibility of a concept consists in this that, if we presuppose it, two contradictory propositions both become false; consequently, as no middle between them is conceivable, nothing at all is thought by that concept.

§ 52c. The first two antinomies, which I call mathematical because they are concerned with the addition or division of the homogeneous, are founded on such a contradictory concept; and hence I explain how it happens that both the thesis and antithesis of the two are false.

When I speak of objects in time and in space, it is not of things in themselves, of which I know nothing, but of things in appearance, that is, of experience, as the particular way of knowing objects which is afforded to man. I must not say of what I think in time or in space, that in itself, and independent of these my thoughts, it exists in space and in time, for in that case I should contradict myself; because space and time, together with the appearances in them, are nothing existing in themselves and outside of my representations, but are themselves only modes of representation, and it is palpably contradictory to say that a mere mode of representation exists without our representation. Objects of the senses therefore exist only in experience, whereas to give them a self-subsisting existence apart from experience or before it is merely to represent to ourselves that experience actually exists apart from experience or before it.

Now if I inquire into the magnitude of the world, as to space and time, it is equally impossible, as regards all my concepts, to declare it infinite or to declare it finite. For neither assertion can be contained in experience, because experience either of an infinite space or of an infinite elapsed time, or again, of the boundary of the world by a void space or by an antecedent void time, is impossible; these are mere Ideas. The magnitude of the world, decided either way, would therefore have to exist in the world itself apart from all experience. But this contradicts the concept of a world of sense, which is merely a complex of the appearances whose existence and connection occur only in our representations, that is, in experience; since this latter is not an object in itself but a mere mode of representation. Hence it follows that, as the concept of an absolutely existing world of sense is self-contradictory, the solution of the problem concerning its magnitude, whether attempted affirmatively or negatively, is always false.

The same holds of the second antinomy, which relates to the division of appearances. For these are mere representations; and the parts exist merely in their representation, consequently in the division—that is, in a possible experience in which they are given—and the division reaches only as far as the possible experience reaches. To assume that an appearance, for example, that of body, contains in itself before all experience all the parts which any possible experience can ever reach is to impute to a mere appearance, which can exist only in experience, an existence previous to experience. In other words, it would mean that mere representations exist before they can be found in our faculty of representation. Such an assertion is self-contradictory, as also every solution of our misunderstood problem, whether we maintain that bodies in themselves consist of an infinite number of parts or of a finite number of simple parts.

§ 53. In the first (the mathematical) class of antinomies the falsehood of the presupposition consists in representing in one concept something self-contradictory as if it were compatible (that is, an appearance as a thing in itself). But, as to the second (the dynamical) class of antinomies, the falsehood of the presupposition consists in representing as contradictory what is compatible; so that while in the former case the opposed assertions were both false, in this case, on the other hand, where they are opposed to one another by mere misunderstanding, they may both be true.

Any mathematical connection necessarily presupposes homogeneity of what is connected (in the concept of magnitude), while the dynamical one by no means requires this. When we have to deal with extended magnitudes all the parts must be homogeneous with one another and with the whole, whereas in the connection of cause and effect homogeneity may indeed likewise be found but is not necessary; for the concept of causality (by means of which something is posited through something else quite different from it) does not in the least require it.

If the objects of the world of sense are taken for things in themselves and the above laws of nature for laws of things in themselves, the contradiction would be unavoidable. So also, if the subject of freedom were, like other objects, represented as mere appearance, the contradiction would be just as unavoidable; for the same predicate would at once be affirmed and denied of the same kind of object in the same sense. But if natural necessity is referred merely to appearances and freedom merely to things in themselves, no contradiction arises if we at the same time assume or admit both kinds of causality, however difficult or impossible it may be to make the latter kind conceivable.

In appearance every effect is an event, or something that happens in time; it must, according to the universal law of nature, be preceded by a determination of the causal act of its cause [11] —this determination being a state of the cause—which it follows according to a constant law. But this determination of the cause to a causal act [12] must likewise be something that takes place or happens; the cause must have begun to act, otherwise no succession between it and the effect could be conceived. Otherwise the effect, as well as the causal act of the cause, would have always existed. Therefore the determination of the cause to act must also have originated among appearances and must consequently, like its effect, be an event, which must again have its cause, and so on; hence natural necessity must be the condition on which efficient causes are determined. Whereas if freedom is to be a property of certain causes of appearances, it must, as regards these, which are events, be a faculty of starting them

[11] [*Kausalität ihrer Ursache.*]
[12] [*Ursache zur Kausalität.*]

spontaneously. That is, it would not require that the causal act of the cause should itself begin [in time], and hence it would not require any other ground to determine its start. But then the cause, as to its causal act, could not rank under time-determinations of its state; that is, it could not be an appearance, but would have to be considered a thing in itself, while only its effects would be appearances.[13] If without contradiction we can think of the beings of understanding as exercising such an influence on appearances, then natural necessity will attach to all connections of cause and effect in the sensuous world; though, on the other hand, freedom can be granted to the cause which is itself not an appearance (but the foundation of appearance). Nature and freedom therefore can without contradiction be attributed to the very same thing, but in different relations—on one side as an appearance, on the other as a thing in itself.

We have in us a faculty which not only stands in connection with its subjective determining grounds [motives] which are the natural causes of its actions and is so far the faculty of a being that itself belongs to appearances, but is also related to objective grounds which are only Ideas so far as they can determine this faculty. This connection is expressed by the word *ought*. This faculty is called "reason," and, so far as we consider a being

[13] The Idea of freedom occurs only in the relation of the intellectual, as cause, to the appearance, as effect. Hence we cannot attribute freedom to matter in regard to the incessant action by which it fills its space, though this action takes place from an internal principle. We can likewise find no notion of freedom suitable to purely rational beings, for instance, to God, so far as his action is immanent. For his action, though independent of external determining causes, is determined in his eternal reason, that is, in the divine *nature*. It is only if *something is to start* by an action, and so the effect occurs in the sequence of time, or in the world of sense (for example, the beginning of the world), that we can put the question whether the causal act of the cause must in its turn have been started or whether the cause can originate an effect without its causal act itself beginning. In the former case, the concept of this activity is a concept of natural necessity; in the latter, that of freedom. From this the reader will see that as I explained freedom to be the faculty of starting an event spontaneously, I have exactly hit the concept which is the problem of metaphysics.

(man) entirely according to this objectively determinable reason, he cannot be considered as a being of sense; this property is a property of a thing in itself, a property whose possibility we cannot comprehend. I mean we cannot comprehend how the *ought* should determine (even if it never has actually determined) its activity and could become the cause of actions whose effect is an appearance in the sensible world. Yet the causality of reason would be freedom with regard to the effects in the sensuous world, so far as we can consider *objective grounds,* which are themselves Ideas, as their determinants. For its action in that case would not depend upon subjective conditions, consequently not upon those of time, and of course not upon the law of nature which serves to determine them, because grounds of reason give the rule universally to actions, according to principles, without influence of the circumstances of either time or place.

What I adduce here is merely meant as an example to make the thing intelligible and does not necessarily belong to our problem, which must be decided from mere concepts independently of the properties which we meet in the actual world.

Now I may say without contradiction that all the actions of rational beings, so far as they are appearances (met with in any experience), are subject to the necessity of nature, but the very same actions, as regards merely the rational subject and its faculty of acting according to mere reason, are free. For what is required for the necessity of nature? Nothing more than the determinability of every event in the world of sense according to constant laws, that is, a reference to cause in the [world of] appearance; in this process the thing in itself at its foundation and its causality remain unknown. But, I say, the law of nature remains, whether the rational being is the cause of the effects in the sensuous world from reason—that is, through freedom— or whether it does not determine them on grounds of reason. For if the former is the case, the action is performed according to maxims, the effect of which as appearance is always con- formable to constant laws; if the latter is the case, and the action not performed on principles of reason, it is subjected to the empirical laws of the sensibility, and in both cases the effects are connected according to constant laws; more than this we do not require or know concerning natural necessity. But in the former case reason is the cause of these laws of nature, and therefore free; in the latter, the effects follow according to mere natural laws of sensibility, because reason does not influence it. But reason itself is not determined on that account by the sensibility (which is impossible) and is therefore free in this case too. Freedom is therefore no hindrance to natural law in appearances; neither does this law abrogate the freedom of the practical use of reason, which is connected with things in themselves, as determining grounds.

Thus practical freedom, namely, the freedom in which reason possesses causality according to objectively determining grounds, is rescued; and yet natural necessity is not in the least curtailed with regard to the very same effects, as appearances. The same remarks will serve to explain what we had to say concerning transcendental freedom and its compatibility with natural necessity in the same subject, but not taken in the same context. For, as to this, every beginning of the action of a being from objective causes regarded as determining grounds is always a *first beginning,* though the same action is in the series of appearances only a *subordinate beginning,* which must be preceded by a state of the cause which determines it and is itself determined in the same manner by another immediately preceding. Thus we are able, in rational beings, or in beings generally so far as their causality is determined in them as things in themselves, to think of a faculty of beginning from themselves a series of states without falling into contradiction with the laws of nature. For the relation of the action to objective grounds of reason is not a time relation; in this case that which determines the causality does not precede in time the action, because such determining grounds represent, not a reference to objects of sense, for example, to causes in the appearances, but to determining causes as things in themselves, which do not fall under conditions of time. And in this way the action, with regard to the causality of reason, can be considered as a first beginning, while in respect to the series of appearances as merely a subordinate beginning. We may therefore without contradiction consider it in the former aspect as free, but in the latter (as it is merely appearance) as subject to natural necessity.

As to the fourth antinomy, it is solved in the same way as the conflict of reason with itself in the third. For, provided the cause *in* the appearance is distinguished from the cause *of* the appearances (so far as it can be thought as a thing in itself), both propositions are perfectly reconcilable: the one, that there is nowhere in the sensuous world a cause (according to similar laws of causality) whose existence is absolutely necessary; the other, that this world is nevertheless connected with a necessary being as its cause (but of another kind and according to another law). The incompatibility of these propositions rests entirely upon the mistake of extending what is valid merely of appearances to things in themselves and in confusing both in one concept.

§ 54. This, then, is the exposition, and this the solution of the whole antinomy in which reason finds itself involved in the application of its principles to the sensible world. The former alone (the mere exposition) would be a considerable service in the cause of our knowledge of human reason, even though the solution might fail fully to satisfy the reader, who has here to combat a natural illusion which has been but recently exposed to him and which he had hitherto always regarded as genuine. For one result at least is unavoidable. As it is quite impossible to prevent this conflict of reason with itself—so long as the objects of the sensible world are taken for things in themselves and not for mere appearances, which they are in fact—the reader is thereby compelled to examine over again the deduction of all our *a priori* knowledge and the proof which I have given of my deduction in order to come to a decision on the question. This is all I require at present; for when in this occupation he shall have thought himself deep enough into the nature of pure reason, those concepts by which alone the solution of the conflict of reason is possible will become sufficiently familiar to him. Without this preparation, I cannot expect an unreserved assent even from the most attentive reader.

III.   The Theological Idea [14]

§ 55.   The third transcendental Idea, which affords matter for the most important but (if pursued only speculatively) transcendent and thereby dialectical use of reason, is the Ideal of pure reason. Reason in this case does not, as with the psychological and the cosmological Ideas, begin from experience and err by exaggerating its grounds in striving to attain, if possible, the absolute completeness of their series. Rather, it totally breaks with experience and from mere concepts of what constitutes the absolute completeness of a thing in general; and thus, by means of the Idea of a most perfect primal Being, it proceeds to determine the possibility and therefore the actuality of all other things. And so the mere presupposition of a Being conceived, not in the series of experience yet for the purposes of experience, for the sake of comprehending its connection, order, and unity—in a word, the Idea—is more easily distinguished from the concept of the understanding here than in the former cases. Hence we can easily expose the dialectical illusion which arises from our making the subjective conditions of our thinking objective conditions of objects themselves, and from making an hypothesis necessary for the satisfaction of our reason into a dogma. As the observations of the *Critique* on the pretensions of transcendental theology are intelligible, clear, and decisive, I have nothing more to add on the subject.

General Remark on the Transcendental Ideas

§ 56.   The objects which are given us by experience are in many respects incomprehensible, and many questions to which the law of nature leads us when carried beyond a certain point (though still quite conformably to the laws of nature) admit of no answer. An example is the question: Why do material things attract one another? But if we entirely quit nature or, in pursuing its combinations, exceed all possible experience, and so

[14] Cf. *Critique of Pure Reason*, "The Transcendental Ideal."

enter the realm of mere Ideas, we cannot then say that the object is incomprehensible and that the nature of things proposes to us insoluble problems. For we are not then concerned with nature or even with given objects, but with mere concepts which have their origin solely in our reason, and with mere beings of thought; and all the problems that arise from our concepts of them must be solved, because of course reason can and must give a full account of its own procedure.[15] As the psychological, cosmological, and theological Ideas are nothing but pure concepts of reason which cannot be given in any experience, the questions which reason asks us about them are put to us, not by the objects, but by mere maxims of our reason for the sake of its own satisfaction. They must all be capable of satisfactory answers, which are given by showing that they are principles which bring our use of the understanding into thorough agreement, completeness, and synthetical unity, and that they thus hold good of experience only, but of experience as a whole.

Although an absolute whole of experience is impossible, the Idea of a whole of knowledge according to principles must impart to our knowledge a peculiar kind of unity, that of a system, without which it is nothing but piecework and cannot be used for proving the existence of a highest purpose (which can only be the general system of all purposes). I do not here refer only to the practical, but also to the highest purpose of the speculative use of reason.

The transcendental Ideas therefore express the peculiar voca-

[15] Herr Platner, in his *Aphorismen*, acutely says (§§ 728, 729), "If reason be a criterion, no concept which is incomprehensible to human reason can be possible. Incomprehensibility has place in what is actual only. Here incomprehensibility arises from the insufficiency of the acquired ideas." It sounds paradoxical, but is otherwise not strange to say that in nature there is much that is incomprehensible (for example, the faculty of reproduction); but if we mount still higher and go even beyond nature, everything again becomes comprehensible. For we then quit entirely the objects which can be given us and occupy ourselves merely about Ideas, in which occupation we can easily comprehend the law that reason prescribes by them to the understanding for its use in experience, because the law is the reason's own production.

tion of reason as a principle of systematic unity in the use of the understanding. Yet if we assume this unity of the mode of knowledge to pertain to the object of knowledge, if we regard that which is merely *regulative* to be *constitutive,* and if we persuade ourselves that we can by means of these Ideas widen our knowledge transcendently or far beyond all possible experience, while it only serves to render experience within itself as nearly complete as possible, that is, to limit its progress by nothing that cannot belong to experience—if we do this, I say—we suffer from a mere misunderstanding in our estimate of the proper role of our reason and of its principles, and a dialectic arises which both confuses the empirical use of reason and sets reason at variance with itself.

CONCLUSION

ON THE DETERMINATION OF THE BOUNDS OF
PURE REASON

§ 57. Having adduced the clearest arguments, it would be
absurd for us to hope that we can know more of any object than
belongs to the possible experience of it or lay claim to the least
knowledge of anything not assumed to be an object of possible
experience which would determine it according to the constitution
it has in itself. For how could we determine anything in this
way, since time, space, and all the concepts of the understanding, and still more all the concepts formed by empirical intuition (perception) in the sensible world, have and can have no
other use than to make experience possible? And if this condition
is omitted from the pure concepts of the understanding, they
do not determine any object and have no meaning whatever.

But it would be, on the other hand, a still greater absurdity
if we conceded no things in themselves or set up our experience
as the only possible mode of knowing things, our intuition of
them in space and in time for the only possible intuition and
our discursive understanding for the archetype of every possible
understanding; for this would be to wish to have the principles
of the possibility of experience considered universal conditions
of things in themselves.

Our principles, which limit the use of reason to possible experience, might in this way become transcendent and the limits
of our reason be set up as limits of the possibility of things in
themselves (as Hume's *Dialogues* may illustrate) if a careful
critique did not guard the bounds of our reason with respect to
its empirical use and set a limit to its pretensions. Skepticism
originally arose from metaphysics and its anarchic dialectic. At
first it might, merely to favor the empirical use of reason, an-
nounce everything that transcends this use as worthless and

deceitful; but by and by, when it was perceived that the very same principles that are used in experience insensibly and apparently with the same right led still further than experience extends, then men began to doubt even the principles of experience. But here there is no danger, for common sense will doubtless always assert its rights. A certain confusion, however, arose in science, which cannot determine how far reason is to be trusted, and why only so far and no farther; and this confusion can only be cleared up and all future relapses obviated by a formal determination, on principle, of the boundary of the use of our reason.

We cannot indeed, beyond all possible experience, form a definite concept of what things in themselves may be. Yet we are not at liberty to abstain entirely from inquiring into them; for experience never satisfies reason fully but, in answering questions, refers us further and further back and leaves us dissatisfied with regard to their complete solution. This anyone may gather from the dialectic of pure reason, which therefore has its good subjective grounds. Having acquired, as regards the nature of our soul, a clear conception of the subject, and having come to the conviction that its manifestations cannot be explained materialistically, who can refrain from asking what the soul really is and, if no concept of experience suffices for the purpose, from accounting for it by a concept of reason (that of a simple immaterial being), though we cannot by any means prove its objective reality? Who can satisfy himself with mere empirical knowledge in all the cosmological questions of the duration and of the magnitude of the world, of freedom or of natural necessity, since every answer given on principles of experience begets a fresh question, which likewise requires its answer and thereby clearly shows the insufficiency of all physical modes of explanation to satisfy reason? Finally, who does not see in the thoroughgoing contingency and dependence of all his thoughts and assumptions on mere principles of experience the impossibility of stopping there? And who does not feel himself compelled, notwithstanding all interdictions against losing himself in transcendent Ideas, to seek rest and contentment, beyond all the concepts which he can vindicate by experience, in the concept of a Being the possibility of the Idea of which cannot be conceived but at the same time cannot be refuted, because it relates to a mere being of the understanding and without it reason must needs remain forever dissatisfied?

Bounds (in extended beings) always presuppose a space existing outside a certain definite place and inclosing it; limits do not require this, but are mere negations which affect a quantity so far as it is not absolutely complete. But our reason, as it were, sees in its surroundings a space for knowledge of things in themselves, though we can never have definite concepts of them and are limited to appearances only.

As long as the knowledge of reason is homogeneous, definite bounds to it are inconceivable. In mathematics and in natural philosophy, human reason admits of limits but not of bounds, namely, it admits that something indeed lies without it, at which it can never arrive, but not that it will at any point find completion in its internal progress. The enlarging of our views in mathematics and the possibility of new discoveries are infinite; and the same is the case with the discovery of new properties of nature, of new powers and laws, by continued experience and its rational combination. But limits cannot be mistaken here, for mathematics refers to appearances only, and what cannot be an object of sensuous intuition, such as the concepts of metaphysics and of morals, lies entirely without its sphere; it can never lead to them, but neither does it require them. There is, therefore, not a continual progress and approximation towards these sciences, and there is not, as it were, any point or line of contact. Natural science will never reveal to us the internal constitution of things, which, though not appearance, yet can serve as the ultimate ground for explaining appearances. Nor does that science require this for its physical explanations. Nay, even if such grounds should be offered from other sources (for instance, the influence of immaterial beings), they must be rejected and not used in the progress of its explanations. For these explanations must only be grounded upon that which as an object of sense can belong to experience, and be brought into connection with our actual perceptions and empirical laws.

But metaphysics leads us towards bounds in the dialectical attempts of pure reason (not undertaken arbitrarily or wantonly, but stimulated thereto by the nature of reason itself). And the transcendental Ideas, as they do not admit of evasion but are never capable of realization, serve to point out to us actually not only the bounds of the pure use of reason, but also the way to determine them. Such is the end and the use of this natural predisposition of our reason, which has brought forth metaphysics as its favorite child, whose generation, like every other in the world, is not to be ascribed to blind chance but to an original germ, wisely organized for great ends. For metaphysics, in its fundamental features, perhaps more than any other science, is placed in us by nature itself and cannot be considered the production of an arbitrary choice or a casual enlargement in the progress of experience from which it is quite disparate.

Reason through all its concepts and laws of the understanding which are sufficient to it for empirical use, that is, within the sensible world, finds in it no satisfaction, because ever-recurring questions deprive us of all hope of their complete solution. The transcendental Ideas which have that completion in view are such problems of reason. But it sees clearly that the sensuous world cannot contain this completion; neither, consequently, can all the concepts which serve merely for understanding the world of sense, for example, space and time, and what we have adduced under the name of pure concepts of the understanding. The sensuous world is nothing but a chain of appearances connected according to universal laws; it has therefore no subsistence by itself; it is not the thing in itself, and consequently must point to that which contains the basis of this appearance, to beings which cannot be known merely as appearances, but as things in themselves. In the knowledge of them alone can reason hope to satisfy its desire for completeness in proceeding from the conditioned to its conditions.

We have above (§§ 33 and 34) indicated the limits of reason with regard to all knowledge of mere beings of thought. Now, since the transcendental Ideas have made it necessary to approach them and thus have led us, as it were, to the spot where the occupied space (namely, experience) touches the void (that of which we can know nothing, namely, *noumena*), we can determine the bounds of pure reason. For in all bounds there is something positive (for example, a surface is the boundary of corporeal space, and is therefore itself a space; a line is a space, which is the boundary of the surface, a point the boundary of the line, but yet always a place in space), but limits contain mere negations. The limits pointed out in those paragraphs are not enough after we have discovered that beyond them there still lies something (though we can never know what it is in itself). For the question now is, What is the attitude of our reason in this connection of what we know with what we do not, and never shall, know? This is an actual connection of a known thing with one quite unknown (and which will always remain so), and though what is unknown should not become in the least more known—which we cannot even hope—yet the concept of this connection must be definite and capable of being rendered distinct.

We must therefore think an immaterial being, a world of understanding, and a Supreme Being (all mere *noumena*), because in them only, as things in themselves, reason finds that completion and satisfaction which it can never hope for in the derivation of appearances from their homogeneous grounds, and because these actually have reference to something distinct from them (and totally heterogeneous), as appearances always presuppose an object in itself and therefore suggest its existence whether we can know more of it or not.

But as we can never know these beings of understanding as they are in themselves, that is, as definite, yet must assume them as regards the sensible world and connect them with it by reason, we are at least able to think this connection by means of such concepts as express their relation to the world of sense. If we represent to ourselves a being of the understanding by nothing but pure concepts of the understanding, we then indeed represent nothing definite to ourselves, and consequently our concept has no significance; but if we think of it by properties borrowed from the sensuous world, it is no longer a being of understanding, but is conceived phenomenally and belongs to the sensible world. Let us take an instance from the notion of the Supreme Being.

The deistic conception is a quite pure concept of reason, but represents only a thing containing all reality, without being able to determine any one reality [in it]; because for that purpose an example must be taken from the world of sense, in which case I should have an object of sense only, not something quite heterogeneous which can never be an object of sense. Suppose I attribute to the Supreme Being understanding, for instance; I have no concept of an understanding other than my own, one that must receive its intuitions by the senses and which is occupied in bringing them under rules of the unity of consciousness. Then the elements of my concept would always lie in the appearance; I should, however, by the insufficiency of the appearance have to go beyond them to the concept of a being which neither depends upon appearances nor is bound up with them as conditions of its determination. But if I separate understanding from sensibility to obtain a pure understanding, then nothing remains but the mere form of thinking without intuition, by which form alone I can know nothing definite and consequently no object. For that purpose I should finally have to conceive another understanding, such as would intuit its objects but of which I have not the least concept, because the human understanding is discursive and can know only by means of general concepts. And the very same difficulties arise if we attribute a will to the Supreme Being, for I have this concept only by drawing it from my inner experience, and therefore from my dependence for satisfaction upon objects whose existence I require; and so the concept rests upon sensibility, which is absolutely incompatible with the pure concept of the Supreme Being.

Hume's objections to deism are weak, and affect only the proofs and not the deistic assertion itself. But as regards theism, which depends on a stricter determination of the concept of the Supreme Being, which in deism is merely transcendent, they are very strong and, as this concept is formed, in certain (in fact in all common) cases irrefutable. Hume always insists that by the mere concept of an original being to which we apply only ontological predicates (eternity, omnipresence, omnipotence) we think nothing definite, and that properties which could yield a concept *in concreto* would have to be superadded. He further insists that it is not enough to say it is cause, but we must explain the nature of its causality, for example, that it is that of an understanding and of a will. He then begins his attacks on the essential point itself, that is, theism, as he had previously directed his battery only against the proofs of deism, an attack which is not very dangerous to it in its consequences. All his dangerous arguments refer to anthropomorphism, which he holds to be inseparable from theism and to make it contradictory in itself; but if the former be abandoned, the latter must vanish with it and nothing remain but deism, of which nothing can come, which is of no value and which cannot serve as any foundation to religion or morals. If this anthropomorphism were really unavoidable, no proofs whatever of the existence of a Supreme Being, even were they all granted, could determine for us the concept of this Being without involving us in contradictions.

If we connect with the command to avoid all transcendent judgments of pure reason the command (which apparently conflicts with it) to proceed to concepts that lie beyond the field of its immanent (empirical) use, we discover that both can subsist together, but only at the boundary of all permitted use of reason. For this boundary belongs to the field of experience as well as to that of the beings of thought, and we are thereby taught how these so remarkable Ideas serve merely for marking the bounds of human reason. On the one hand, they give warning not boundlessly to extend knowledge of experience, as if nothing but world remained for us to know, and yet, on the other hand, not to transgress the bounds of experience and to think of judging about things beyond them as things in themselves.

But we stop at this boundary if we limit our judgment merely to the relation which the world may have to a Being whose very concept lies beyond all the knowledge which we can attain within the world. For we then do not attribute to the Supreme Being any of the properties in themselves by which we represent objects of experience, and thereby avoid *dogmatic* anthropomorphism;

but we attribute them to the relation of this Being to the world and allow ourselves a *symbolical* anthropomorphism, which in fact concerns language only and not the object itself.

If I say that we are compelled to consider the world *as if* it were the work of a Supreme Understanding and Will, I really say nothing more than that a watch, a ship, a regiment, bears the same relation to the watchmaker, the shipbuilder, the commanding officer as the world of sense (or whatever constitutes the substratum of this complex of appearances) does to the unknown, which I do not hereby know as it is in itself but as it is for me, that is, in relation to the world of which I am a part.

§ 58.   Such a cognition is one of analogy and does not signify (as is commonly understood) an imperfect similarity of two things, but a perfect similarity of relations between two quite dissimilar things.[1] By means of this analogy, however, there remains a concept of the Supreme Being sufficiently determined *for us,* though we have left out everything that could determine it absolutely or *in itself;* for we determine it as regards the world and hence as regards ourselves, and more do we not require. The attacks which Hume makes upon those who would determine this concept absolutely, by taking the materials for so doing from themselves and the world, do not affect us; and he cannot object

[1] There is, for example, an analogy between the juridical relation of human actions and the mechanical relation of moving forces. I never can do anything to another man without giving him a right to do the same to me on the same conditions; just as no mass can act with its moving forces on another mass without thereby occasioning the other to react equally against it. Here right and moving force are quite dissimilar things, but in their relation there is complete similarity. By means of such an analogy, I can obtain a notion of the relation of things which absolutely are unknown to me. For instance, as the promotion of the welfare of children $(= a)$ is to the love of parents $(= b)$, so the welfare of the human species $(= c)$ is to that unknown character in God $(= x)$, which we call love; not as if it had the least similarity to any human inclination, but because we can suppose its relation to the world to be similar to that which things of the world bear one another. But the concept of relation in this case is a mere category, namely, the concept of cause, which has nothing to do with sensibility.

to us that we have nothing left if we give up the objective anthropomorphism of the concept of the Supreme Being.

For let us assume at the outset (as Hume in his *Dialogues* makes Philo grant Cleanthes), as a necessary hypothesis, the deistic concept of the First Being, in which this Being is thought by the mere ontological predicates of substance, of cause, and so on. This must be done because reason, actuated in the sensible world by mere conditions which are themselves always conditional, cannot otherwise have any satisfaction; and it therefore can be done without falling into anthropomorphism (which transfers predicates from the world of sense to a Being quite distinct from the world) because those predicates are mere categories which, though they do not give a determinate concept of that Being, yet give a concept not limited to any conditions of sensibility. Thus nothing can prevent our predicating of this Being a causality through reason with regard to the world, and thus passing to theism, without being obliged to attribute to this Being itself this kind of reason, as a property inherent in it. For as to the former, the only possible way of prosecuting the use of reason (as regards all possible experience in complete harmony with itself) in the world of sense to the highest point is to assume a supreme reason as a cause of all the connections in the world. Such a principle must be quite advantageous to reason and can hurt it nowhere in its application to nature. As to the latter, reason is thereby not transferred as a property to the First Being in itself, but only to its relation to the world of sense, and so anthropomorphism is entirely avoided. For nothing is considered here but the cause of the form of reason which is perceived everywhere in the world, and reason is indeed attributed to the Supreme Being so far as it contains the ground of this form of reason in the world, but according to analogy only—that is, so far as this expression shows merely the relation which the Supreme Cause, unknown to us, has to the world in order to determine everything in it conformably to reason in the highest degree. We are thereby kept from using reason as an attribute for the purpose of conceiving God, but not from conceiving the world in such a manner as is necessary to have the greatest possible use of reason within it according to principle. We thereby acknowledge that the Supreme Being is quite inscrutable and even unthinkable in any definite way as to what it is in itself. We are thereby kept, on the one hand, from making a transcendent use of the concepts which we have of reason as an efficient cause (by means of the will), in order to determine the Divine Nature by properties which are only borrowed from human nature, and from losing ourselves in gross and extravagant notions; and, on the other hand, from deluging the contemplation of the world with hyperphysical modes of explanation according to our notions of human reason which we transfer to God, and so from losing for this contemplation its proper rôle, according to which it should be a rational study of mere nature and not a presumptuous derivation of its appearances from a Supreme Reason. The expression suited to our feeble notions is: we conceive the world *as if* it came, in its existence and internal plan, from a Supreme Reason. By this, on the one hand, we know the constitution which belongs to the world itself without pretending to determine the nature of its cause in itself; and, on the other hand, we transfer the ground of this constitution (of the form of reason in the world) upon the *relation* of the Supreme Cause to the world, without finding the world sufficient by itself for that purpose.[2]

Thus the difficulties which seem to oppose theism disappear by combining with Hume's principle, "not to carry the use of reason dogmatically beyond the field of all possible experience," this other principle, which he quite overlooked, "not to consider the field of experience as one which bounds itself in the eyes of our reason." The *Critique of Pure Reason* here points out the true mean between dogmatism, which Hume combats, and skep-

[2] I may say that the causality of the Supreme Cause holds the same place with regard to the world that human reason does with regard to its works of art. Here the nature of the Supreme Cause itself remains unknown to me; I only compare its effects (the order of the world), which I know, and their conformity to reason to the effects of human reason, which I also know; and hence I term the former "reason," without attributing to it on that account what I understand in man by this term, or attaching to it anything else known to me as its property.

ticism, which he would substitute for it—a mean which is not like others the⁴ we find advisable to determine for ourselves, as it were mechanically (by adopting something from one side and something from the other), and by which nobody is taught a better way, but such a one as can be precisely determined on principles.

§ 59. At the beginning of this note I made use of the metaphor of a boundary, in order to establish the limits of reason in regard to its suitable use. The world of sense contains merely appearances, which are not things in themselves; but the understanding, because it recognizes that the objects of experience are mere appearances, must assume that there are things in themselves, namely, *noumena*. In our reason both are comprehended, and the question is, How does reason proceed to set boundaries to the understanding as regards both these fields? Experience, which contains all that belongs to the sensible world, does not bound itself; it only proceeds in every case from the conditioned to some other equally conditioned object. That which bounds it must lie quite without it, and this is the field of the pure beings of the understanding. But this field, so far as the *determination* of the nature of these beings is concerned, is an empty space for us; and apart from dogmatically defined concepts, we cannot pass beyond the field of possible experience. But as a boundary itself is something positive, which belongs to that which lies within as well as to the space that lies without the given content, it is still an actual positive cognition which reason only acquires by enlarging itself to this boundary, yet without attempting to pass it because it there finds itself in the presence of an empty space in which it can conceive forms of things, but not things themselves. But the setting of a boundary to the field of the understanding by something which is otherwise unknown to it is still a cognition which belongs to reason even at this point, and by which it is neither confined within the sensible nor strays beyond it, but only limits itself, as befits the knowledge of a boundary, to the relation between that which lies beyond it and that which is contained within it.

Natural theology is such a concept at the boundary of human

reason, being constrained to look beyond this boundary to the Idea of a Supreme Being (and, for practical purposes, to that of an intelligible world also), not in order to determine anything relatively to this pure being of the understanding, and thus to determine something that lies beyond the world of sense, but in order to guide the use of reason within it according to principles of the greatest possible (theoretical as well as practical) unity. For this purpose, it makes use of the reference of the world of sense to an independent reason as the cause of all its connections. Thereby it does not just *invent* a being, but, as beyond the sensible world there must be something that can be thought only by the pure understanding, it determines that something in this particular way, though only of course by analogy.

And thus there remains our original proposition, which is the *résumé* of the whole *Critique:* "Reason by all its *a priori* principles never teaches us anything more than objects of possible experience, and even of these nothing more than can be known in experience." But this limitation does not prevent reason from leading us to the objective boundary of experience, namely, to the relation to something which is not itself an object of experience but is the ground of all experience. Reason does not, however, teach us anything concerning the thing in itself; it only instructs us as regards its own complete and highest use in the field of possible experience. But this is all that can be reasonably desired in the present case, and with it we have cause to be satisfied.

§ 60. Thus we have fully exhibited metaphysics, in its subjective possibility, as it is actually given in the natural predisposition of human reason and in that which constitutes the essential end of its pursuit. Though we have found that this merely natural use of such a predisposition of our reason, if no discipline arising only from a scientific critique bridles and sets limits to it, involves it in transcendent and specious inferences and really conflicting dialectical inferences, and this fallacious metaphysics is not only unnecessary as regards the promotion of our knowledge of nature but even disadvantageous to it, there yet remains a problem worthy of investigation, which is to find out the natural ends intended by this disposition to transcendent concepts in our nature, because everything that lies in nature must be originally intended for some useful purpose.

Such an inquiry is of a doubtful nature, and I acknowledge that what I can say about it is conjecture only, like every speculation about the ultimate ends of nature. Such conjecture may be allowed me here, for the question does not concern the objective validity of metaphysical judgments but our natural predisposition to them, and therefore does not belong to the system of metaphysics but to anthropology.

When I compare all the transcendental Ideas, the totality of which constitutes the proper problem of natural pure reason, compelling it to quit the mere contemplation of nature, to transcend all possible experience, and in this endeavor to produce the thing (be it knowledge or fiction) called metaphysics, I think I perceive that the aim of this natural tendency is to free our concepts from the fetters of experience and from the limits of the mere contemplation of nature so far as at least to open to us a field containing mere objects for the pure understanding which no sensibility can reach, not indeed for the purpose of speculatively occupying ourselves with them (for there we can find no ground to stand on), but in order that practical principles [may be assumed as at least possible];[3] for practical principles, unless they find scope for their necessary expectation and hope, could not expand to the universality which reason unavoidably requires from a moral point of view.

So I find that the psychological Idea (however little it may reveal to me the nature of the human soul, which is elevated above all concepts of experience), shows the insufficiency of these concepts plainly enough and thereby deters me from materialism, a psychological concept which is unfit for any explanation of nature and which moreover confines reason in practical respects. The cosmological Ideas, by the obvious insufficiency of all possible knowledge of nature to satisfy reason in its legitimate inquiry, serve in the same manner to keep us from naturalism,

[3] [Kant's clause is incomplete. The translation here follows the suggestion of B. Erdmann—L.W.B.]

which asserts nature to be sufficient for itself. Finally, all natural necessity in the sensible world is conditional, as it always pre-supposes the dependence of things upon others, and uncondi-tional necessity must be sought only in the unity of a cause different from the world of sense. But as the causality of this cause, in its turn, were it merely nature, could never render the existence of the contingent (as its consequent) comprehensible, reason frees itself by means of the theological Idea from fatalism (both as a blind natural necessity in the coherence of nature itself, without a first principle, and as a blind causality of this principle itself) and leads to the concept of a cause possessing freedom or of a Supreme Intelligence. Thus the transcendental Ideas serve, if not to instruct us positively, at least to destroy the narrowing assertions of materialism, of naturalism, and of fatalism, and thus to afford scope for the moral Ideas beyond the field of speculation. These considerations, I should think, explain in some measure the natural predisposition of which I spoke.

The practical value, which a merely speculative science may have, lies without the bounds of this science, and can therefore be considered as a scholium merely, and like all scholia does not form part of the science itself. This application, however, surely lies within the bounds of philosophy, especially of philosophy drawn from the pure sources of reason, where its speculative use in metaphysics must necessarily be at one with its practical use in morals. Hence the unavoidable dialectic of pure reason, considered in metaphysics as a natural tendency, deserves to be explained not as a mere illusion, which is to be removed, but also, if possible, as a natural provision as regards its end, though this task, a work of supererogation, cannot justly be assigned to metaphysics proper.

The solutions of these questions which are treated in the *Critique* [4] should be considered a second scholium, which, how-ever, has a greater affinity with the subject of metaphysics. For

---

[4] *Critique of Pure Reason,* "Regulative Use of the Ideas of Pure Reason."

there certain rational principles are expounded which determine
a priori the order of nature or rather of the understanding, which
seeks nature's laws through experience. They seem to be constitutive and legislative with regard to experience, though they
spring from pure reason, which cannot be considered, like the
understanding, as a principle of possible experience. Now whether
or not this harmony rests upon the fact that, just as nature
does not inhere in appearances or in their source (the sensibility)
itself, but only in the relation of the latter to the understanding,
a thorough unity in applying the understanding to bring about
an entirety of all possible experience (in a system) can only
belong to the understanding when in relation to reason, with the
consequence that experience is in this way mediately subordinate
to the legislation of reason—this question may be discussed by
those who desire to trace the nature of reason even beyond its
use in metaphysics, into the general principles, which will make
a history of nature in general systematic. I have presented this
task as important, but not attempted its solution in the book
itself.[5]

And thus I conclude the analytical solution of the main question which I had proposed: "How is metaphysics in general
possible?" by ascending from the data of its actual use, as shown
in its consequences, to the grounds of its possibility.

[5] Throughout in the *Critique* I never lost sight of the plan not to
neglect anything, were it ever so recondite, that could render the
inquiry into the nature of pure reason complete. Everybody may
afterward carry his research as far as he pleases, when he has been
merely shown what yet remains to be done. This can reasonably be
expected of him who has made it his business to survey the whole
field, in order to consign it to others for future cultivation and allot-
ment. And to this branch both the scholia belong, which will hardly
recommend themselves because of their dryness to amateurs, and
hence are added here for connoisseurs only.

SOLUTION OF THE GENERAL QUESTION
OF THE *PROLEGOMENA*

HOW IS METAPHYSICS POSSIBLE AS SCIENCE?

METAPHYSICS, as a natural disposition of reason, is actual; but if considered by itself alone (as the analytical solution of the third principal question showed), dialectical and illusory. If we think of taking principles from it, and in using them follow the natural, but on that account not less false, illusion, we can never produce science, but only a vain dialectical art, in which one school may outdo another but none can ever acquire a just and lasting approbation.

In order that as a science metaphysics may be entitled to claim, not mere fallacious plausibility, but insight and conviction, a critique of reason itself must exhibit the whole stock of *a priori* concepts, their division according to their various sources (sensibility, understanding, and reason), together with a complete table of them, the analysis of all these concepts, with all their consequences, and especially the possibility of synthetical knowledge *a priori* by means of a deduction of these concepts, the principles and the bounds of their application, all in a complete system. Critique, therefore, and critique alone contains in itself the whole well-proved and well-tested plan, and even all the means, required to establish metaphysics as a science; by other ways and means it is impossible. The question here, therefore, is not so much how this performance is possible as how to set it going and to induce men of clear heads to quit their hitherto perverted and fruitless cultivation for one that will not deceive, and how such a union for the common end may best be directed.

This much is certain, that whoever has once tasted critique will be ever after disgusted with all dogmatic twaddle which he formerly had to put up with because his reason had to have something and could find nothing better for its support.

Critique stands in the same relation to the common metaphysics of the schools as chemistry does to alchemy, or as astronomy to the astrology of the fortune teller. I pledge myself that nobody who has thought through and grasped the principles of critique, even in these *Prolegomena* only, will ever return to that old and sophistical pseudo-science; but will rather with a certain delight look forward to metaphysics, which is now indeed in his power, requiring no more preparatory discoveries and affording permanent satisfaction to reason at last. For here is an advantage upon which, of all possible sciences, metaphysics alone can with certainty reckon: that it can be brought to such completion and fixity as to be in need of no further change or be subject to any augmentation by new discoveries; because here reason has the sources of its knowledge in itself, not in objects and their observation,[1] by which its stock of knowledge could be further increased. When, therefore, it has exhibited the fundamental laws of its faculty completely and so definitely as to avoid all misunderstanding, there remains nothing further which pure reason could know *a priori;* nay, there is no ground even to raise further questions. The sure prospect of knowledge so definite and so compact has a peculiar charm, even though we should set aside all its advantages, of which I shall hereafter speak.

All false art, all vain wisdom, lasts its time but finally destroys itself, and its highest culture is also the epoch of its decay. That this time is come for metaphysics appears from the state into which it has fallen among all learned nations, despite all the zeal with which other sciences of every kind are prosecuted. The old arrangement of our university studies still preserves its shadow. Now and then an academy of science tempts men by offering prizes to write some essay on it, but it is no longer numbered among the rigorous sciences; and let anyone judge for himself how a sophisticated man, if he were called a great metaphysician, would receive the compliment, which may be well meant but is scarcely envied by anybody.

Yet, though the period of the downfall of all dogmatic meta-

---

[1] [*Anschauung.*]

physics has undoubtedly arrived, we are yet far from being able to say that the period of its regeneration is come by means of a thorough and complete critique of reason. All transitions from a tendency to its contrary pass through the stage of indifference, and this moment is the most dangerous for an author but, in my opinion, the most favorable for the science. For when party spirit has died out by a total dissolution of former connections, minds are in the best state to listen to several proposals for an organization according to a new plan.

When I say that I hope these *Prolegomena* will excite investigation in the field of critique and afford a new and promising object to sustain the general spirit of philosophy, which seems on its speculative side to want sustenance, I can imagine beforehand that everyone whom the thorny paths of my *Critique* have tired and put out of humor will ask me upon what I found this hope. My answer is: upon the irresistible law of necessity.

That the human mind will ever give up metaphysical researches is as little to be expected as that we, to avoid inhaling impure air, should prefer to give up breathing altogether. There will, therefore, always be metaphysics in the world; nay, everyone, especially every reflective man, will have it and, for want of a recognized standard, will shape it for himself after his own pattern. What has hitherto been called metaphysics cannot satisfy any critical mind, but to forego it entirely is impossible; therefore a *Critique of Pure Reason* itself must now be attempted or, if one exists, investigated and brought to the full test, because there is no other means of supplying this pressing want which is something more than mere thirst for knowledge.

Ever since I have come to know critique, whenever I finish reading a book of metaphysical contents which, by the preciseness of its notions, by variety, order, and an easy style, was not only entertaining but also helpful, I cannot help asking, "Has this author indeed advanced metaphysics a single step?" The learned men whose works have been useful to me in other respects and always contributed to the culture of my mental powers will, I hope, forgive me for saying that I have never been able to find either their essays or my own less important ones (though self-

love may recommend them to me) to have advanced the science
of metaphysics in the least.

There is a very obvious reason for this: metaphysics did not
then exist as a science, nor can it be gathered piecemeal; but its
germ must be fully preformed in critique. But, in order to prevent all misconception, we must remember what has been already
said—that, by the analytical treatment of our concepts, the
understanding gains indeed a great deal; but the science of
metaphysics is thereby not in the least advanced, because these
dissections of concepts are nothing but the materials from which
the intention is to carpenter our science. Let the concepts of substance and of accident be ever so well dissected and determined;
all this is very well as a preparation for some future use. But if
we cannot prove that in all which exists the substance endures
and only the accidents vary, our science is not the least advanced
by all our analyses.

Metaphysics has hitherto never been able to prove *a priori*
either this proposition or that of sufficient reason, still less any
more complex theorem such as belongs to psychology or cos-
mology, or indeed any synthetical proposition. By all its analyzing,
therefore, nothing is affected, nothing obtained or forwarded;
and the science, after all this bustle and noise, still remains as
it was in the days of Aristotle, though there were far better prep-
arations for it than of old if only the clue to synthetical cognitions
had been discovered.

If anyone thinks himself offended, he is at liberty to refute
my charge by producing a single synthetical proposition belonging to metaphysics which he would prove dogmatically *a priori;*
for until he has actually performed this feat I shall not grant
that he has truly advanced the science, even if this proposition
should be sufficiently confirmed by common experience. No demand can be more moderate or more equitable and, in the
(inevitably certain) event of its nonperformance, no assertion
more just than that hitherto metaphysics has never existed as a
science.

But there are two things which, in case the challenge be accepted, I must deprecate: first, trifling about probability and con-

jecture, which are suited as little to metaphysics as to geometry; and secondly, a decision by means of the magic wand of so-called common sense, which does not convince everyone but accommodates itself to personal peculiarities.

For as to the former, nothing can be more absurd than in metaphysics, a philosophy from pure reason, to think of grounding our judgments upon probability and conjecture. Everything that is to be known *a priori* is thereby announced as apodictically certain, and must therefore be proved in this way. We might as well think of grounding geometry or arithmetic upon conjectures. As to the calculus of probabilities in the latter, it does not contain probable but perfectly certain judgments concerning the degree of the possibility of certain cases under given uniform conditions, which, in the sum of all possible cases, must infallibly happen according to the rule, though the rule is not sufficiently definite with respect to every single instance. Conjectures (by means of induction and of analogy) can be suffered in an empirical science of nature only, yet even there at least the possibility of what we assume must be quite certain.

The appeal to common sense is even more absurd—if anything more absurd can be imagined—when it is a question of concept and principles claimed as valid, not in so far as they hold with regard to experience, but beyond the conditions of experience. For what is common sense? It is normal good sense, so far it judges right. But what is normal good sense? It is the faculty of the knowledge and use of rules *in concreto,* as distinguished from the speculative understanding, which is a faculty of knowing rules *in abstracto.* Common sense can hardly understand the rule that every event is determined by means of its cause and can never comprehend it in its generality. It therefore demands an example from experience; and when it hears that this rule means nothing but what it always thought when a pane was broken or a kitchen utensil missing, it then understands the principle and grants it. Common sense, therefore, is only of use so far as it can see its rules (though they actually are *a priori*) confirmed by experience; consequently to comprehend them *a priori,* or independently of experience, belongs to the speculative understanding and lies quite beyond the horizon of common sense. But the province of metaphysics is entirely confined to the latter kind of knowledge, and it is certainly a bad sign of common sense to appeal to it as a witness, for it cannot here form any opinion whatever, and men look down upon it with contempt until they are in straits and can find in their speculation neither advice nor help.

It is a common subterfuge of those false friends of common sense (who occasionally prize it highly, but usually despise it) to say that there must surely be at all events some propositions which are immediately certain and of which there is no occasion to give any proof, or even any account at all, because we otherwise could never stop inquiring into the grounds of our judgments. But if we except the principle of contradiction, which is not sufficient to show the truth of synthetical judgments, they can never adduce, in proof of this privilege, anything else indubitable which they can immediately ascribe to common sense, except mathematical propositions, such as twice two make four, between two points there is but one straight line, etc. But these judgments are radically different from those of metaphysics. For in mathematics I can by thinking itself construct whatever I represent to myself as possible by a concept: I add to the first two the other two, one by one, and myself make the number four, or I draw in thought from one point to another all manner of lines, equal as well as unequal; yet I can draw one only which is like itself in all its parts. But I cannot, by all my power of thinking, extract from the concept of a thing the concept of something else whose existence is necessarily connected with the former; for this I must call in experience. And though my understanding furnishes me *a priori* (yet only in reference to possible experience) with the concept of such a connection (that is causation), I cannot exhibit it, like the concepts of mathematics, by intuiting it *a priori,* and so show its possibility *a priori.* This concept, together with the principles of its application, always requires, if it shall hold *a priori*—as is requisite in metaphysics—a justification and deduction of its possibility, because we cannot otherwise know how far it holds good and whether it can be used in experience only or beyond it also.

Therefore in metaphysics, as a speculative science of pure reason, we can never appeal to common sense, but may do so only when we are forced to surrender it and to renounce all pure speculative knowledge which must always be theoretical cognition,[2] and thereby under some circumstances to forego metaphysics itself and its instruction for the sake of adopting a rational faith which alone may be possible for us, sufficient to our wants, and perhaps even more salutary than knowledge itself. For in this case the state of affairs is quite altered. Metaphysics must be science, not only as a whole, but in all its parts; otherwise it is nothing at all; because, as speculation of pure reason, it finds a hold only on common convictions. Beyond its field, however, probability and common sense may be used justly and with advantage, but on quite special principles, the importance of which always depends on their reference to practical life.

This is what I hold myself justified in requiring for the possibility of metaphysics as a science.

APPENDIX

On What Can Be Done to Make Metaphysics as a Science Actual

SINCE all the ways heretofore taken have failed to attain the goal, and since without a preceding critique of pure reason it is not likely ever to be attained, the present attempt has a right to an accurate and careful examination, unless it be thought more advisable to give up all pretensions to metaphysics, to which, if men but would consistently adhere to their purpose, no objection can be made.

---

[2] [*Ein Wissen.*]

If we take the course of things as it is, not as it ought to be, there are two sorts of judgments: (1) one a judgment which precedes investigation (in our case one in which the reader from his own metaphysics pronounces judgment on the *Critique of Pure Reason,* which was intended to discuss the very possibility of metaphysics); (2) the other a judgment subsequent to investigation. In the latter, the reader is enabled to ignore for a while the consequences of the critical researches that may be repugnant to his formerly adopted metaphysics, and first examines the grounds whence those consequences are derived. If what common metaphysics propounds were demonstrably certain, as is the case with the theorems of geometry, the former way of judging would hold good. For if the consequences of certain principles are repugnant to established truths, these principles are false and without further inquiry to be repudiated. But if metaphysics does not possess a stock of indisputably certain (synthetical) propositions, and should it even be the case that there are a number of them, which, though among the most plausible, are by their consequences in mutual conflict, and if no sure criterion of the truth of peculiarly metaphysical (synthetical) propositions is to be met with in it, then the former way of judging is not admissible, but the investigation of the principles of the *Critique* must precede all judgments as to its value.

A Specimen of a Judgment of the Critique Prior to Its Examination

Such a judgment is to be found in the *Göttingische gelehrte Anzeigen,* in the supplement to the third part, of January 19, 1782, pages 40 *et seq.*

When an author who is familiar with the subject of his work and endeavors to present his independent reflections in its elaboration falls into the hands of a reviewer who, in his turn, is keen enough to discern the points on which the worth or worthlessness of the book rests, who does not cling to words but goes to the heart of the subject, sifting and testing the principles which the author takes as his point of departure,[1] the severity of the judgment may indeed displease the author, but the public does not care, as it gains thereby. And the author himself may be contented, as an opportunity of correcting or explaining his positions is afforded to him at an early date by the examination of a competent judge, in such a manner that if he believes himself fundamentally right, he can remove in time any stumbling block that might hurt the success of his work.

I find myself, with my reviewer, in quite another position. He seems not to see at all the real matter of the investigation with which (successfully or unsuccessfully) I have been occupied. It is either impatience at thinking out a lengthy work, or vexation at a threatened reform of a science in which he believed he had brought everything to perfection long ago, or, what I am reluctant to suspect, real narrow-mindedness that prevents him from ever carrying his thoughts beyond his school metaphysics. In short, he passes impatiently in review a long series of propositions, of which, without knowing their premises, one can understand nothing, intersperses here and there his censure, the reason of which the reader understands just as little as the propositions against which it is directed; and hence [his report] can neither serve the public nor damage me in the judgment of experts. I should, for these reasons, have passed over this judgment altogether, were it not that it may afford me occasion for some explanations which may in some cases save the readers of these *Prolegomena* from a misconception.

In order to take a position from which my reviewer could most easily set the whole work in a most unfavorable light, without venturing to trouble himself with any special investigation, he begins and ends by saying: "This work is a system of transcendental (or, as he translates it, of higher [2]) idealism."

---

[1] [Omitting *nicht*.—Vorländer.]

[2] By no means "higher." High towers and metaphysically great men resembling them, round both of which there is commonly much wind, are not for me. My place is the fruitful bathos of experience; and the word "transcendental," the meaning of which is so often explained by me but not once grasped by my reviewer (so carelessly has he regarded

A glance at this line soon showed me the sort of criticism that I had to expect, much as though the reviewer were one who had never seen or heard of geometry, having found a Euclid and coming upon various figures in turning over its leaves, were to say, on being asked his opinion of it: "The work is a textbook of drawing; the author introduces a peculiar terminology, in order to give dark, incomprehensible directions, which in the end teach nothing more than what everyone can effect by a fair natural accuracy of eye, etc."

Let us see, in the meantime, what sort of an idealism it is that goes through my whole work, although it does not by a long way constitute the soul of the system.

The dictum of all genuine idealists, from the Eleatic school to Bishop Berkeley, is contained in this formula: "All knowledge through the senses and experience is nothing but sheer illusion, and only in the ideas of the pure understanding and reason is there truth."

The principle that throughout dominates and determines my idealism, is on the contrary: "All knowledge of things merely from pure understanding or pure reason is nothing but sheer illusion, and only in experience is there truth."

But this is directly contrary to idealism proper. How came I then to use this expression for quite an opposite purpose, and how came my reviewer to see it everywhere?

The solution of this difficulty rests on something that could have been very easily understood from the general bearing of the work if the reader had only desired to understand it. Space and time, together with all that they contain, are not things in themselves or their qualities, but belong merely to the appear-

everything), does not signify something passing beyond all experience but something that indeed precedes it *a priori*, but that is intended simply to make knowledge of experience possible. If these conceptions overstep experience, their employment is termed "transcendent," which must be distinguished from the immanent use, that is, use restricted to experience. All misunderstandings of this kind have been sufficiently guarded against in the work itself, but my reviewer found his advantage in misunderstanding me.

ances of the things in themselves. Up to this point I am one in confession with the above idealists. But these, and among them more particularly Berkeley, regarded space as a mere empirical representation that, like the appearances it contains, is, together with its determinations, known to us only by means of experience or perception. I, on the contrary, prove in the first place that space (and also time, which Berkeley did not consider) and all its *a priori* determinations can be known by us, because, no less than time, it inheres in us as a pure form of our sensibility before all perception or experience and makes all intuition of the form, and therefore all appearances, possible. It follows from this that, as truth rests on universal and necessary laws as its criteria, experience, according to Berkeley, can have no criteria of truth because its phenomena [3] (according to him) have nothing *a priori* at their foundation, whence it follows that experience is nothing but sheer illusion; whereas with us, space and time (in conjunction with the pure concept of the understanding) prescribe their law to all possible experience *a priori* and, at the same time, afford the certain criterion for distinguishing truth from illusion therein.[4]

My so-called (properly critical) idealism is of quite a special character, in that it subverts the ordinary idealism and in that only through it all *a priori* knowledge, even that of geometry, receives objective reality, which, without my demonstrated ideality of space and time, could not be maintained by the most zealous realists. This being the state of the case, I could wish, in order to avoid all misunderstanding, to have named this conception of mine otherwise, but to alter it altogether is probably impossible.

---

[3] Idealism proper always has a mystical tendency, and can have no other, but mine is solely designed for the purpose of comprehending the possibility of our *a priori* knowledge of objects of experience, which is a problem never hitherto solved or even suggested. In this way all mystical idealism falls to the ground, for (as may be seen in Plato) it inferred from our cognitions *a priori* (even from those of geometry) another intuition different from that of the senses (namely, an intellectual intuition), because it never occurred to anyone that the senses themselves might intuit *a priori*.

[4] [*Erscheinungen.*]

It may be permitted me however, in future, as has been above intimated, to term it "formal" or, better still, "critical" idealism, to distinguish it from the dogmatic idealism of Berkeley and from the skeptical idealism of Descartes.

Beyond this, I find nothing remarkable in the judgment of my book. The reviewer makes sweeping criticisms, a mode prudently chosen, since it does not betray one's own knowledge or ignorance; a single thorough criticism in detail, had it touched the main question, as is only fair, would have exposed either my error or my reviewer's measure of insight into this species of research. It was, moreover, not a badly conceived plan, in order at once to take from readers (who are accustomed to form their conceptions of books from newspaper reports) the desire to read the book itself, to pour out in one breath a number of passages in succession which, torn from their connection with their premises and explanations, must necessarily sound senseless, especially considering how antipathetic they are to all school-metaphysics; to exhaust the reader's patience *ad nauseam,* and then, having made me acquainted with the lucid proposition that persistent illusion is truth, to conclude with the crude paternal moralization: to what end, then, the quarrel with accepted language; to what end, and whence, the idealistic distinction? A judgment which seeks all that is characteristic of my book, first supposed to be metaphysically heterodox, in a mere innovation of the nomenclature proves clearly that my would-be judge has understood nothing of the subject and, in addition, has not understood himself.[5]

My reviewer speaks like a man who is conscious of important

[5] The reviewer often fights with his own shadow. When I oppose the truth of experience to dream, he never thinks that I am here speaking simply of the well-known *somnio objective sumto* of the Wolffian philosophy, which is merely formal, and with which the distinction between sleeping and waking is in no way concerned—a distinction which can indeed have no place in a transcendental philosophy. For the rest, he calls my deduction of the categories and table of the principles of the understanding "common well-known axioms of logic and ontology, expressed in an idealistic manner." The reader need only consult these *Prolegomena* upon this point to convince himself that a more miserable and historically incorrect judgment could hardly be made.

and superior insight which he keeps hidden, for I am aware of nothing recent with respect to metaphysics that could justify his tone. But he should not withhold his discoveries from the world, for there are doubtless many who, iike myself, have not been able to find in all the fine things that have for long past been written in this department anything that has advanced the science by so much as a finger's breadth; we find indeed the giving a new point to definitions, the supplying of lame proofs with new crutches, the adding to the crazy-quilt of metaphysics fresh patches or changing its pattern. But all this is not what the world requires. The world is tired of metaphysical assertions; it wants [to know] the possibility of this science, the sources from which certainty therein can be derived, and certain criteria by which it may distinguish the dialectical illusion of pure reason from truth. To this the critic seems to possess a key, otherwise he would never have spoken out in such a high tone.

But I am inclined to suspect that no such requirement of the science has ever entered his thoughts, for in that case he would have directed his judgment to this point, and even a mistaken attempt in such an important matter would have won his respect. If that be the case, we are once more good friends. He may penetrate as deeply as he likes into his metaphysics, without any one hindering him; oniy as concerns that which lies outside metaphysics, its sources, which are to be found in reason, he cannot form a judgment. That my suspicion is not without foundation is proved by the fact that he does not mention a word about the possibility of synthetic knowledge *a priori*, the special problem upon the solution of which the fate of metaphysics wholly rests and upon which my *Critique* (as well as the present *Prolegomena*) entirely hinges. The idealism he encountered and which he hung upon was only taken up in the doctrine as the sole means of solving the above problem (although it received its confirmation on other grounds), and hence he must have shown either that the above problem does not possess the importance I attribute to it (even in these *Prolegomena*) or that, by my conception of appearances, it is either not solved at all or can be better solved in another way; but I do not find a word of this in the criticism. The reviewer, then, understands nothing of my work and possibly also nothing of the spirit and essential nature of metaphysics itself; and it is not, what I would rather assume, the hurry of a reviewer to finish his review, incensed at the labor of plodding through so many obstacles, that threw an unfavorable shadow over the work lying before him and made its fundamental features unrecognizable.

There is a good deal to be done before a learned journal, it matters not with what care its writers may be selected, can maintain its otherwise well-merited reputation in the field of metaphysics as elsewhere. Other sciences and branches of knowledge have their standard. Mathematics has it in itself, history and theology in profane or sacred books, natural science and the art of medicine in mathematics and experience, jurisprudence in law books, and even matters of taste in the examples of the ancients. But for the judgment of the thing called metaphysics, the standard has yet to be found. I have made an attempt to determine it, as well as its use. What is to be done, then, until it be found when works of this kind have to be judged of? If they are of a dogmatic character, one may do what one likes; no one will play the master over others here for long before someone else appears to deal with him in the same manner. If, however, they are critical in character, not indeed with reference to other works but to reason itself, so that the standard of judgment cannot be assumed but has first of all to be sought for, then, though objection and blame may indeed be permitted, yet a certain degree of leniency is indispensable, since the need is common to us all and the lack of the necessary insight makes the high-handed attitude of judge unwarranted.

In order, however, to connect my defense with the interest of the philosophical commonwealth, I propose a test, which must be decisive as to the mode whereby all metaphysical investigations may be directed to their common purpose. This is nothing more than what mathematicians have done in establishing the advantage of their methods by competition. I challenge my critic to demonstrate, as is only just, on *a priori* grounds, in his own way, any single really metaphysical proposition asserted by him.

Being metaphysical, it must be synthetical and known *a priori* from concepts, but it may also be any one of the most indispensable propositions, as, for instance, the principle of the persistence of substance or of the necessary determination of events in the world by their causes. If he cannot do this (silence however is confession), he must admit that, since metaphysics without apodictic certainty of propositions of this kind is nothing at all, its possibility or impossibility must before all things be established in a critique of pure reason. Thus he is bound either to confess that my principles in the *Critique* are correct, or he must prove their invalidity. But as I can already foresee that, confidently as he has hitherto relied on the certainty of his principles, when it comes to a strict test he will not find a single one in the whole range of metaphysics he can boldly bring forward, I will concede to him an advantageous condition, which can only be expected in such a competition, and will relieve him of the *onus probandi* by laying it on myself.

He finds in these *Prolegomena* and in my *Critique*[6] eight propositions, of which one in each pair contradicts the other, but each of which necessarily belongs to metaphysics, by which it must either be accepted or rejected (although there is not one that has not in its time been assumed by some philosopher). Now he has the liberty of selecting any one of these eight propositions at his pleasure and accepting it without any proof, of which I shall make him a present, but only one (for waste of time will be just as little serviceable to him as to me), and then of attacking my proof of the opposite proposition. If I can save this one and at the same time show that, according to principles which every dogmatic metaphysics must necessarily recognize, the opposite of the proposition adopted by him can be just as clearly proved, it is thereby established that metaphysics has an hereditary failing not to be explained, much less set aside, until we ascend to its birthplace, pure reason itself. And thus my *Critique* must either be accepted or a better one take its place; at least

[6] [The reference is to the theses and antitheses of the antinomies.—L.W.B.]

it must be studied, which is the only thing I now require. If, on the other hand, I cannot save my demonstration, then a synthetic proposition *a priori* from dogmatic principles is to be reckoned to the score of my opponent, and I shall deem my impeachment of ordinary metaphysics unjust and pledge myself to recognize his stricture on my *Critique* as justified (although this would not be the consequence by a long way). To this end it would be necessary, it seems to me, that he should step out of his incognito. Otherwise I do not see how it could be avoided that, instead of dealing with one, I should be honored or besieged by several challenges coming from anonymous and unqualified opponents.

Proposals as to an Investigation of the "Critique" Upon Which a Judgment May Follow

I feel obliged to the learned public even for the silence with which it for a long time honored my *Critique,* for this proves at least a postponement of judgment and some supposition that, in a work leaving all beaten tracks and striking out on a new path, in which one cannot at once perhaps so easily find one's way, something may perchance lie from which an important but at present dead branch of human knowledge may derive new life and productiveness. Hence may have originated a solicitude for the as yet tender shoot, lest it be destroyed by a hasty judgment. A specimen of a judgment, delayed for the above reasons, is now before my eye in the *Gothaische gelehrte Zeitung,* the thoroughness of which—disregarding my praise, which might be suspicious—every reader will himself perceive from the clear and unperverted presentation of a fragment of one of the first principles of my work.

Since an extensive structure cannot be judged of as a whole from a hurried glance, I suggest that it be tested piece by piece from the ground up, and in this, the present *Prolegomena* may fitly be used as a general outline with which the work itself may occasionally be compared. This notion, if it were founded on nothing more than my conceit of importance, such as vanity commonly attributes to all of one's own productions, would be immodest and would deserve to be repudiated with indignation. But now the interests of speculative philosophy have arrived at the point of total extinction, while human reason hangs upon them with inextinguishable affection; and only after having been ceaselessly deceived, does it vainly attempt to change this into indifference.

In our thinking age, it is not to be supposed but that many deserving men would use any good opportunity of working for the common interest of the more and more enlightened reason, if there were only some hope of attaining the goal. Mathematics, natural science, laws, arts, even morality, etc., do not completely fill the soul; there is always a space left over reserved for pure and speculative reason, the emptiness of which prompts us to seek in vagaries, buffooneries, and mysticism for what seems to be employment and entertainment, but what actually is mere pastime undertaken in order to deaden the troublesome voice of reason, which, in accordance with its nature, requires something that can satisfy it and does not merely subserve other ends or the interests of our inclinations. A consideration, therefore, which is concerned only with reason as it exists for it itself has, as I may reasonably suppose, a great fascination for everyone who has attempted thus to extend his conceptions, and I may even say a greater fascination than any other theoretical branch of knowledge, for which he would not willingly exchange it because here all other branches of knowledge and even purposes must meet and unite themselves in a whole.

I offer, therefore, these *Prolegomena* as a sketch and textbook for this investigation, and not the work itself. Although I am even now perfectly satisfied with the latter as far as contents, order, and mode of presentation, and the care that I have expended in weighing and testing every sentence before writing it down are concerned (for it has taken me years to satisfy myself fully, not only as regards the whole, but in some cases even as to the sources of one particular proposition); yet I am not quite satisfied with my exposition in some sections of the Doctrine of

Elements,[7] as for instance in the deduction of the concepts of the understanding or in the chapter on the paralogisms of pure reason, because a certain diffuseness takes away from their clearness, and in place of them what is here said in the *Prolegomena* respecting these sections may be made the basis of the test.[8]

It is the boast of the Germans that, where steady and continuous industry are requisite, they can carry things farther than other nations. If this opinion be well founded, an opportunity, a task, presents itself the successful issue of which we can scarcely doubt and in which all thinking men can equally take part, though they have hitherto been unsuccessful in accomplishing it and in thus confirming the above good opinion. This is chiefly because the science in question is of so peculiar a kind that it can all at once be brought to completion and to that enduring state beyond which it can never be developed, in the least degree enlarged by later discoveries, or changed if we leave out of account adornment by greater clearness in some places or additional uses. This is an advantage no other science has or can have, because there is none so fully isolated and independent of others and so exclusively concerned with the faculty of cognition pure and simple. And the present moment seems not to be unfavorable to my expectation, for just now, in Germany, no one seems to know wherewith to occupy himself, apart from the so-called useful sciences, so as to pursue not mere play but a business possessing an enduring purpose.

To discover how the endeavors of the learned may be united in such a purpose I must leave to others. In the meantime, it is not my intention to persuade anyone merely to follow my propositions or even to flatter me with the hope that he will do so; but attacks, repetitions, limitations, or confirmation, completion, and extension, as the case may be, should be appended. If the matter be but investigated from its foundation, it cannot

[7] [The first part of the *Critique of Pure Reason*, the other being the Methodology.—L.W.B.]

[8] [These sections were almost completely rewritten in the second edition of the *Critique* (1787), though the new deduction of the categories does not follow the argument of the *Prolegomena*.—L.W.B.]

fail that a system, albeit not my own, shall be erected that shall be a possession for future generations for which they may have reason to be grateful.

It would lead us too far here to show what kind of metaphysics may be expected when the principles of criticism have been perfected and how, though the old false feathers have been pulled out, it need by no means appear poor and reduced to an insignificant figure but may be in other respects richly and respectably adorned. But other and great uses which would result from such a reform strike one immediately. The ordinary metaphysics had its uses, in that it sought out the elementary concepts of the pure understanding in order to make them clear through analysis and definite through definitions. In this way it was a training for reason, in whatever direction it might be turned. But this was all the good it did. The service was subsequently effaced when it favored conceit by venturesome assertions, sophistry by subtle distinctions and adornment, and shallowness by the ease with which it decided the most difficult problems by means of a little school wisdom, which is only the more seductive the more it has the choice, on the one hand, of taking something from the language of science and, on the other, from that of popular discourse—thus being everything to everybody but in reality nothing at all. By criticism, however, a standard is given to our judgment whereby knowledge may be with certainty distinguished from pseudo-science and firmly founded, being brought into full operation in metaphysics—a mode of thought extending by degrees its beneficial influence over every other use of reason, at once infusing into it the true philosophical spirit. But the service that metaphysics performs also for theology, by making it independent of the judgment of dogmatic speculation and thereby assuring it completely against the attacks of all such opponents, is certainly not to be valued lightly. For ordinary metaphysics, although it promised theology much advantage, could not keep this promise, and by summoning speculative dogmatics to its assistance did nothing but arm enemies against itself. Mysticism, which can prosper in a rationalistic age only when it hides itself behind a system of school metaphysics, under the protection of which it may venture to rave with a semblance of rationality, is driven from theology, its last hiding place, by critical philosophy. Last, but not least, it cannot be otherwise than important to a teacher of metaphysics to be able to say with universal assent that what he expounds is *science*, and that by it genuine services will be rendered to the commonweal.

INDEX

134